Lessons Learned in Retirement

Retiring with purpose and passion

D0874987

Lessons Learned in Retirement: Retiring with purpose and passion
©2022 Mariella Hoy

First edition

Library and Archives Canada Cataloguing in Publication is available
ISBN 978-1-7387172-0-0 (paperback)

Design and Layout: Barry Millar
Cover Illustration: *Setting Out: Three Mile Lake 2* by Helen Hoy
Cover Design: Tracey Ujfalussy

Nestledown Books
Printed in Canada

What a glorious romp through what can range anywhere from a desperately challenging to an exhilaratingly inspirational transition — from what we are in our working lives to who we hope to be in our "retirement" lives. Navigating these issues with humour, compassion, wisdom, insight, vulnerability, and her trademark "organizational lists," Mariella's cleverly-crafted mentoring manual is a comforting and welcoming guide on how to "see and claim our power" and create "purpose, passion, and well-being" during these most important and fulfilling years of our lives. A thoroughly enjoyable and valuable read!

John P. Brown (he/him),
Legal and Strategic Advisor, Indigenous Initiatives,
McCarthy Tétrault LLP

Foreword

Ten years ago, my Ivey Business School classmates Mariella Hoy and Helen Hillman invited me to attend a pre-retirement workshop they had created. Even though my wife and I were not close to thinking about retirement — other than long-term financial planning — we decided to attend. I knew Mariella to be very capable. She was the president of the undergraduate business students all those years ago, and had won a peer-voted merit award upon graduation. I was confident it would be a worthwhile workshop.

In the opening presentation, Mariella and Helen spoke about how their research showed that, after the honeymoon phase, a significant number of new retirees were not satisfied with their new life. How could that be possible? Hearing about this malaise at that life stage piqued our interest. We really dug in for the rest of the day. I still have the sheets they asked us to fill out at the end, to help guide us when we reached retirement. After the workshop, my wife and I continued to reflect on what would work best for each of us in that long-distant future state.

I retired 5 years ago, after 35 great years with IBM, where I had many roles, globally and in Canada. In my last role I had 8,000 people in my organization. I was fortunate to represent the company/sector in external settings, creating many large partnership projects with governments and universities. This led to being on 10 external boards, including chairing the Canadian Chamber of Commerce in 2013/14. My work was busy — so much so that my work colleagues expressed the firm belief that I would never be able to 'retire.' Little did they know that I had the workshop learning from Mariella.

Although I was able to 'call my own shot' when I retired, I knew I'd have to focus in earnest on a mix of areas that had very little to do with finances. I had connected with many retirees who expressed the same dissatisfaction that Mariella had described — loss of identity, status, direction — and it reinforced that this feeling is very common. In our unique way, and in part because of what we learned in the workshop, my wife and I decided to concentrate on creating purpose, passion, learning, and health in our retirement.

I have had an amazing start to retirement. We've travelled, volunteered (both of us at Southlake Hospital, where I am presently Board Chair), learned and taught (I was a Western University adjunct professor for 2 years) and am now co-founder of an AI company. I golf, work out regularly, and have returned to piano and

French lessons. Of course, kids and grandkids are top priority and we spend lots of time with them. I have also faced challenges. I lost two brothers and my parents, and I dealt with health scares. I'm learning to be resilient and to accept what life offers.

I am so pleased that Mariella has written this book. The stories, successes, challenges, and — especially — the lessons offered by so many contributors provide a huge array of experiences that deepen the valuable insights we gained 10 years ago. I will be sure to send out many copies to my friends who are retiring — or holding off that decision because 'I don't know what I would do with myself.' Now, instead of trying to explain, I'll simply send them a copy of this guide, to help them create conditions to have a "soft, warm current at their backs" as they retire.

Patrick Horgan, Retired
Vice President, Manufacturing, Development and Operations (COO)
IBM Canada

I dedicate this book to my sister Teresa, a consummate dreamer, who fed my curiosity to learn more about dreaming, and yearning, and wishing. When I was 35 years old, she wrote a note to me: *Such mysterious things, wishes are, aren't they?*

This book is also for those of you toying with the idea of making your silent wishes work for you in retirement.

Table of Contents

Why this book is necessary

The transition into retirement is like the start of a kayak trip: Whether you were sent fondly on your way by waving, well-meaning colleagues, or rudely thrown off the dock, arms and legs flailing, the hard realization slams home that your emotional well-being is solely in your own hands. As the dock you were tethered to for so long fades from view, you turn your eyes forward, only to see a fog engulfing you and your small boat. A panic starts thrumming low in your throat.

As we prepare for retirement, we can feel exposed, at risk, and unsure of our future. No matter how much financial planning we do in preparation, and no matter how exhilarated we may be about leaving work behind, our confidence can be assaulted by the cold unknown.

I recently spoke with a strong, independent woman considering retirement. During our conversation, she mentioned that she had kayaked in places all around the world. When last in Greenland, a whale suddenly rose up under her kayak and lifted her out of the water. She was exhilarated. When she talked of her retirement, though, she said that the personal side of retirement had her "perplexed" and she had no idea how to handle it. It struck me that retirement had her more unsettled than the wild whale ride.

As Rose, one of the contributing writers in this book, said, "If you have been in the habit of operating reasonably well within a set of parameters, you sometimes get very used to working within the box. Suddenly the sides of the box are flattened and it is all up to you."

Frank, another contributing writer, told of his feeling of exposure: "Despite feeling ebullient about leaving work behind, I was feeling a bit like a turtle out of its shell. I no longer had my cloak of status, my shield of twice-monthly paycheques, and my trusty electronics that served me so well in battling never-ending tasks. I was alone with myself and was feeling uneasy staring myself in the eyes."

It's no real surprise to me that retirement can perplex, even panic, those about to launch forth. Leaving our secure world of work and heading into the haze that hides our destination is discombobulating. The sunny, calm waters we thought would be our retirement now appear choppy. Instead of our usual charted course, this journey is unmapped. Our relaxed competence is threatened and we're not used to being unsure.

But that's okay. It's okay to sit in this unsettling place for awhile. As we sit and cogitate, the mists will clear from our minds and we'll see a way forward. We'll soon be able to handle retirement confidently, knowing our value in the world, and gleeful about our new identities. We'll be full of purpose and passion, in a learning frame of mind, ready to give up our old work life, and open to great possibilities.

That is what this book is about: getting us safely launched, on a charted course to where we long to be, full speed ahead, and mighty pleased with ourselves.

A soft, warm current at your back

In this book are the stories of retirees who faced the emotional and social challenges most often dealt with in retirement. As well, I'll share my favourite nuggets of learning, distilled from years of retirement coaching, facilitating retirement workshops, reading, gathering stories, and conducting surveys. My main nuggets focus on three important components of well-being and happiness. It's not enough to know we want a happy retirement; we need to know how to make that happen. For that reason, I've included the theories of well-being, purpose, and passion.

This is not a financial planning book. The book's focus is emotional and social well-being in retirement. Its immediate goal is to soften the period of disorientation that can come as we transition into retirement, reducing or eliminating depression, anxiety, and grief. Its broader goal is to get us closer to our ideal retirement, faster... by guiding us to become exactly who we want to be, doing all that we want to do. Simply put, it's about shopping for delight.

For those of you thinking about retiring or recently retired, I hope the stories and information you read will inspire, enlighten, and embolden you. For those of you well into retirement who sense that something important is missing in your lives, I trust you'll find some of the missing pieces on these pages.

I love the retirement phase of life. The whole world stops briefly and asks, "What do you really want?" Psychologist Rick Hanson put it eloquently when he said, "Imagine your deepest wants like a soft warm current at your back, gently and powerfully carrying you forward along the long road ahead."[1]

The stories and information in this book are to enable that soft, warm current at your back, allowing you to probe the question of what you really, really want.

---

1 Hanson, R. (n.d.). See Deep Wants. Retrieved, with permission, August 12, 2022, from https://www.rickhanson.net/see-deep-wants/

Who am I?

My name is Mariella Hoy and I'm a life coach, female, age 66. For most of my adult life I've been known as Mariella Vigneux, but recently I reclaimed my birth surname, Hoy, exasperated with the gender inequality of 'maiden' names. I've been married only once, but the 45 years have more than made up for any missed experiences. I have two grown children who both still love me, so I figure my parenting guesswork paid off. After attaining a Masters in Business Administration, I gained humility, work experience, and knowledge while working with IBM and Public Health. I now specialize in retirement life coaching. The arrogance of the Life Coach title embarrasses me, but the recommended title of Certified Professional Coach — weighted with its ambiguity and self-importance — also causes me to wriggle. Whatever the title, I love my work. I've spent the last 15 years riding shotgun for people who were figuring out what to do with the rest of their lives. I'm gratified that my clients have gone away happier than when they arrived.

I work out of a home office in a log house on 50 acres of bush, at the dead-end of a road not far from a small city in Ontario, Canada. To save money during the winter (scarcity thinking), I turn down the propane furnace and heat my office with a woodstove. With the cat curled up by the stove and snow falling on the crabapple tree outside the window, it can be quite cozy.

Despite all I've learned about retirement, I'm perplexed about my own retirement well-being. I dither and ponder. This insecurity has provided much enjoyment for my brother-in-law, who I poked and prodded through years of his own pre-retirement angst. My dithering puts an unholy gleam in his eye. The presumption of me writing a retirement self-help book puts an unholy gleam in mine.

What is causing my insecurity? Maybe I'm afraid to make the leap because it was late in life when I finally figured out what I wanted to be when I grew up. I haven't had long enough being that grownup. Maybe it's because I distrust the stirrings that say I'm ready to give up something I love. Whatever the reason, I haven't been saved from the disorientation that this phase of life can bring.

How this book came about

Although my personal uncertainty about retirement is one reason for this book (you write what you want to learn about), the main reason is because so many people I talk to are anxious to know how to bridge what looks like a treacherous gap between their current existence and what they hope to build in retirement life: a sense of purpose, passionate activities, warm relationships, well-being, and a feeling of fulfillment. What they see in financial and healthcare advertising are whitewashed, stereotypical retirees in wheat-coloured knit sweaters, with blindingly white teeth, smiling complacently while riding bicycles built for two. Where is the pain, grit, confusion, and quirky individualism? Where are the answers they crave? The financial planning and pension seminars cover well-being topics as if they are the gingerbread on the house, instead of the concrete foundation.

Another driver behind the book is that it provides a way to finally tease out the answers to questions that have danced through my consciousness since I was a kid.

1. What do you want to be when you grow up?
2. What makes you happy?
3. What changes can you make to create a better life for yourself?

These questions have fascinated me. They've shaped my choices for work and play and guided my conversations with pretty much anyone I've bumped into over the course of my life. And one thing has led to another.

Flagging tape led to retirement coaching

If you look back on your life as a kid, you'll find character traits that can act as flagging tape along the trail to where you would be happiest in life.

The earliest flagging tape I remember was when I was perched on the roof of our house spying on the neighbours. I was about 12 years old and wanted to be a detective. I also remember sitting at the family dinner table, a boardroom table purchased by my dad to hold his family of 12. (My parent's Irish Catholicism blessed them with 11 kids, configured as four sets of twins and 'The Three Stooges.' The eldest twins were only 7½ years older than the youngest.) Anyway, I remember holding a spoon to my face like a microphone and asking my siblings and parents, in turn, penetrating questions, like "What was one good thing and what was one bad thing that happened to you today?" Okay, not penetrating questions, but I remember really wanting to know the answers. As a young woman, I read career planning books, such as *You can be whatever you want* and *What Color is Your Parachute.* In my 20s, as I made my way through 5 years of business school, I gravitated to the Human Resources, Organizational Behaviour, and Communications courses. My choice of university program — business — was made by the process of elimination: what did I not want to study. At IBM, although I was in a technical job, I loved the employee career planning and other HR documents. I kept them for years, taking them out periodically to admire them. Over the years since, I collected aptitude tests, leadership models, and personality assessments.

When I was 50, I finally figured out what I wanted to be when I grew up. I wanted to be someone who worked one-on-one with people on their big life issues.

I spent 1½ years with Adler International Learning, a coach training program affiliated with the University of Toronto. In 2006, I founded Crabapple Coaching, a one-person coaching practice.

In true coach-like fashion, I wasn't on some misguided crusade to tell my clients what to do with their lives. I was, rather, fascinated by what they would learn about themselves, what made them happy, and what they wanted to be when they grew up. I thrived on witnessing the changes made to better their lives. (I apologize to my children and first clients for jeopardizing their well-being with my early attempts at coaching.)

Over the years, I realized that, as people near retirement, a cauldron of emotions starts bubbling. It's half terror and half enthusiasm. Retirement struck me as the perfect time to answer those fascinating questions: What do you want to be when you grow up? What makes you happy? What changes can you make to create a better life for yourself?

In the retirement stage of life, usually the burden of having to make a living is gone. The amount of savings we'll have for our retirement has already been determined. If we've had children, generally they have left home and are making their own life decisions. We've had a lifetime to figure out our strengths and weaknesses. We likely have a sense of what we value, what we like, and what we don't like. It's an ideal time to figure out what makes us really come alive. It is for these reasons that I chose to focus my coaching practice on the retirement age and stage of life.

Scary abysses led to the workshop

Retirement is a transition for which many are unprepared. Financial planning is available, but I knew that not much help was being offered to those considering retirement who wanted to explore the non-monetary questions, the important stuff like well-being, happiness, and creating purpose and passion in life.

Also, when faced with retirement we can suddenly confront some scary abysses. I spoke with a man who was retiring after decades working for the same organization. He was distressed about retirement because he had no partner, no children, no close friends, no hobbies, and he was moving to a new town. A woman whose prominent husband was retiring, found herself suddenly retiring as his unpaid social secretary and homemaker. She saw retirement as desolation. I talked with several people who felt shockwaves in their marriages, now that retirement was setting their house of cards teetering. I also spoke with a high-powered professional at the top of her game, overworked, overachieving, courted in her field, but desperate to retire, and at a very young age. Her sister told her she'd be dead within the year if she retired, like a racehorse banished to the pasture. Such scary times for so many people.

Since most financial retirement workshops weren't successfully providing answers to questions about emotional and social well-being, I decided that a different kind of workshop was needed.

Knowing little at that time about retirement, I immersed myself in books and studies about aging well, retirement well-being, the stages of adult development, life transition theory, positive psychology, and happiness.

I took great care to ensure that the new workshop would meet the needs of people who were either thinking about retiring or newly retired. My Learning Needs Assessment included in-depth and key informant interviews. I sought advice from a Dialogue Education specialist, a professor of family studies, a financial-services professional, a therapist who specializes in couples counselling, business owners/ leaders, and others. Based on the needs outlined and the advice given, a business school survivor and friend, Helen Hillman, and I developed the workshop: *Retiring with Purpose and Passion*. We tested our results in a pilot workshop, then delivered our workshop to various organizations and groups around Ontario, always incorporating what we learned from our participants into future workshops.

Learning through others' struggles led to the newsletter

The workshop was well-received and appreciated. However, I kept thinking about the adage that we *learn best through the stories of others*. We learn best through other's struggles, experiences, and wisdom. Working collaboratively with past clients, past workshop participants, friends, and family, I started collecting retirement stories. Every contributor was asked to tell what they had learned from their journey into retirement. Their stories were full of insights and hard-earned lessons.

Each month, I published one or two of these stories in an online newsletter called *Retiring with Purpose and Passion*. Supporting the personal retirement stories were articles presenting theories, research studies, and statistics that showed how to age well and how to create meaning and well-being in retirement. I also added my own musings and those of coaching colleagues.

The newsletter ran for 4 years and became a place where people could learn, exchange observations, and have their thoughts and feelings normalized and validated. With the help of 42 contributing writers, I've posted 170 articles, not to mention the treasures offered by the many Doggerel Cup Contest entrants, survey respondents, people who posted comments on the blog, and our editors.

What a riotous, far-roaming newsletter! Tales of purpose and passion, disorientation, the art of recovery, love, money fears, wattles and wrinkles, loss, Bob Dylan, and groundhogs. Lists and blank pages, onions, unexpected job loss, job burnout, creativity, great expectations, monkeys, retirement trepidation, and spiders.

We bounced around. Partners, grandchildren, daily structure, and self-determination. Old key rings, dreams, downsizing, graveyards, protecting our personal space, sleeping in, and the anguish of a friend. Giving something back, exchanging cash for time, hip surgery, the puritan work ethic, hospices, healthy aging, balance, just saying 'no,' and drunken matadors.

And on... to creating a new identity, inertia, grief, getting to a full stop, sharing chores, bagpipes, vanity, stripping down to the essentials, and liver and onions. And let's not forget mortality, resilience, chronic illness, co-living, contentment, legacy, and tomato sandwiches. How far and wide we travelled together!

By this point, 4 years after the first newsletter, I was completely absorbed in the world of retirement. I was coaching individuals, facilitating workshops, and editing the stories of retirees for the newsletter. I was also learning about how people fared in retirement, and it wasn't all good news. Statistics and studies showed many retirees sailing happily into the sunset, yet there were too many tales of capsizing, wrong turns, and rough voyages.

Startling retirement outcomes led to this book

Retirement is one of the biggest life-transitions we go through. It can affect almost everything: how much money we have, our identity, our routines each day, who we see, our sense of purpose, and even when we sleep. Yet, many of us are unprepared, not understanding how we'll create well-being and happiness in the next stage of our lives. In the first year or two of retirement, many people are surprised by the impact of the changes. They may be staggered by feelings of loneliness and depression. One person was so stressed by retirement that she signed up for stress management classes. That's totally understandable. Retirement usually spans 20 to 40 years, a daunting prospect if most of life's structures and sense of purpose are suddenly gone. So, it is worth spending some thought on how to create a fulfilling post-work life.

It can take many years of considering retirement before we are ready to take the leap. I find that, generally, people take about 5 years to retire — to get to the day when they say, "Sayonara! I'm out of here!"

What is disconcerting is that about one in four retirees is likely to feel confused and troubled after the retirement honeymoon. Sometimes this disorientation can last for years. It can be an anxiety-provoking time. And, although some disorientation is useful for determining what one really wants, it would be better for the retiree, their family, and their friends if the confusion and perplexity did not drag on too long.

When we do finally retire, the top predictor of how well we will adjust to our new retired state is called 'Conditions of Exit.' The conditions of exit from our career are things like choosing our retirement date, having a phased retirement in which we work part time, having time to prepare, going to a retirement workshop, being given a retirement party, and feeling valued as we leave.

But here's the rub. A startling percentage of people retire unexpectedly. They have little or no control over their conditions of exit.

A recent poll revealed that while 55% of pre-retirees expect to know their retirement date at least a year in advance, only 39% of those retired said this was the case. More concerning, 16% of retirees said they had no warning at all.[2]

For years I have been reading polls that outline the reasons why people retired. Just under half of those who left careers for reasons beyond their control retired for heath reasons or to provide caregiving to a family member. Others left at the employer's request. Some quit voluntarily, because they felt out of step with the corporate culture, the direction the organization was heading, or the value placed on their contribution to the workplace.

Whether because of being laid off, an illness, the need to care for a loved one, or becoming fed up, sudden termination of work can be a shocking event. We've had that cruelly brought home to us by the COVID-19 pandemic, which has messed with our anticipated retirement dates, either through job loss, reduced working hours, or extended working years. Sudden job loss for older workers can become permanent, as jobs prospects dwindle. Some have had to close their businesses. Others nearing retirement have chosen to continue working, to make up for the shrinkage of their retirement nest egg. Either way, control of the conditions of exit has flown out the window for many.

---

2 Ipsos (2020, January 16). *Retirement Doesn't Always Go as Planned: RBC/Ipsos Poll*. Retrieved August 9, 2022, from https://www.ipsos.com/en-ca/news-polls/ Retirement-Does-Not-Always-Go-as-Planned

Even without the trials of unexpected or postponed retirement, the retirement phase of life offers many challenges. What happens when we give up our identity, title, power, security, income, roles, status, and recognition? Who are we then? How do we manage the turmoil of joy, sadness, fear, relief, resistance, surprise, anger, and anxiety? What will replace the companionship we had with our work colleagues all those years? How do we structure our days when our daily habits are suddenly gone, when we no longer have a path to follow, when we have no clock or calendar to guide us? What will replace the sense of purpose our careers gave us? How will we adjust to being at home alone or with our spouses all day, every day?

These challenges can make retirement a disconcerting time.

In addition, many of us will face one or more special tests during our transition into retirement. For example, we might move to a new community, be involved in the divorce process, have to adjust to substantially less income, or face a death in the family. Complicated times!

How do we lessen the disenchantment and disequilibrium that can happen as we adjust to our new state? What are the tactics for getting our heads on straight about retirement? Where is the manual for retiring gracefully? Where is the playbook?

A book was crying out to be written. I could see that people wanted support and I was in a position to help. That and my big sister told me to write a book. So, I did. This is it.

How to read this book

Please consider this book your own private retirement coaching, with the added benefits of lessons learned from a bunch of seasoned retirees, snapshots into the retirement process from an "unambitious overachiever," just enough theory to let you know what is important in creating well-being and happiness, plus some quick-reference tools to have handy on your journey.

As you read, you'll be prompted to probe the question of what you really, really want and encouraged to make your retirement as irresistible as possible.

With these ideas in mind, the book is laid out in three sections.

1: Ten Emotional and Social Challenges Faced in Retirement

Out of the morass of retirement questions with which we wrestle as we near retirement and throughout retirement, I discovered clear themes. I've grouped those themes according to the most common emotional and social challenges people face.

The first section of this book is dedicated to these challenges, as seen through the stories of people already retired. (Some of these people asked that their identities not be revealed. All the stories are real.)

Along with the tales of retirement from our contributors, I added my own stories and insights into retirement well-being.

I hope that you will relate to the struggles, stories, and insights in a way that lets you say, "Yes, that is true. I understand that." May they give you clarity, ideas, and inspiration.

Self-coaching questions

At break points throughout the book, you'll find self-coaching questions, which you can use to address your own situation as it relates to the topic under discussion.

Following Frank into retirement

A treat is waiting for you at the end of each topic and each section. Here you'll find stories from Following Frank into Retirement, a popular series of articles starting 5 months before Frank's retirement, and then periodically after retirement, until Frank has 4 years of retirement under his belt. Frank gives us a lively account of what is going on in his head as he progresses through the retirement stages.

Describing himself as an unambitious overachiever, a middle-of-the-road kind of guy, his priorities in life are "family-first, work-second, and Frank-third." Frustrated with his job and deeply desiring retirement, Frank is worried about having enough money. In his stories, he shares his thoughts about bagpipes, money, dental plans, fulfillment, money, lawn mowers, life, and money.

Even if you're not concerned about money in retirement, you'll enjoy watching Frank stickhandle his way to the finish line and beyond.

2: Three Components for Well-Being and Happiness in Retirement

In the second section of the book, I present three components of well-being, with the theories and statistics which underpin them. They describe ways of living that set the conditions necessary for happiness to occur more often. I think of them as the root vegetables of retirement.

3: Some Final Thoughts

I've put together some quick references — tools to keep handy over the coming months — such as a cheat sheet for tackling the challenges, steps to take when preparing for retirement, and a summary of the book's main points. As well, this section contains what I hope are some thoughts to hearten you and get you raring to go. Lastly, the final word goes to Frank, 4 years into his retirement.

Gems

As I already mentioned, for 4 years I published tales of retirement each month in an online newsletter called *Retiring with Purpose and Passion*. At the end of each year, to commemorate a year of published newsletters, the editing team would choose the best bits of wisdom and humour from the contributing writers, looking for universal truths. You'll find these gems in large quotation marks at the end of most chapters.

Now, it is time for you to launch into the stories and information that will provide a soft, warm current at your back, gently guiding you to a retirement full of purpose, passionate activities, warm relationships, well-being, and fulfillment. Pleasant journey!

1

Ten Emotional and Social Challenges Faced in Retirement

Photo: Kati Finell, Bigstock.com

I don't know about you, but I learn best from the personal stories of others going through similar experiences. For that reason — and because it was crazy good fun — I collected over 100 tales of retirement, stories of what it was like to go through the retirement process. I requested these stories from friends, family, and workshop participants, and published their tales in a newsletter over the course of four years. I was intrigued to hear about challenges retirees face.

I asked the contributing writers to consider the following questions:

- How might your story inspire, inform, or embolden people who are considering retirement?
- What have you struggled with, or still struggle with, as you progressed into and through retirement?
- What ideas might you have to offer people (retired or not yet retired)?
- How did you find contentment in retirement? How did you create purpose, passion and well-being?
- What rants or gripes do you have about your retirement experience or the stereotypes you've come up against?
- How is your life experience unique and intriguing?
- What's fun, outrageous, or bizarre? What made you laugh, get mad, get sad, or go crazy?

I was thrilled with the resulting articles. The writers were funny, perceptive, honest, thoughtful, and generous.

Now, I've recently noticed a subtle teasing from some of my many siblings about my tendency to organize information and make lists. In my defense, it is sometimes useful. (And they do it too!) Anyway, I found it a useful 'talent' when I sieved through these 100 or so tales of retirement, looking for common retirement challenges for this book. Ten common challenges emerged:

1 *Dealing with unexpected retirement*

2 *Creating a new identity*

3 *Rebuilding routines*

4 *Adapting to illness and limitations*

5 *Confronting death*

6 *Reasserting positive emotions and a good frame of mind*

7 *Finding meaning and well-being in retirement*

8 *Adjusting relationships at home*

9 *Struggling with the creative urge*

10 *Balancing work and play*

Unfortunately, from the bounty of stories I could only choose a few for this book... those that best illustrate the top 10 challenges faced. At least these stories are finally finding the larger audience they deserve.

To these tales of retirement, I've added my own stories and insights into retirement well-being.

I hope the stories fill you with ideas, inspire you, and help you clarify your retirement plans.

At the end of each topic are self-coaching questions, which you can apply to your own situation. On these question pages, you might like to jot down insights from each story, for later reflection.

"

It was easy for me to retire. I hate rushing in the morning!

– Maryse

"

Dealing with Unexpected Retirement

As mentioned in the opening of this book, a startling number of people retire unexpectedly. They are suddenly laid off or fired. Or they get sick or are required for caregiving. Some get fed up and quit in frustration. What a shock to the system for these reluctant retirees, a tumultuous ride into retirement.

I know what it's like to be forced out of a job. I had my reputation shredded, my mental health assaulted, and my source of income whisked away, all in a 10-month period. That's how long I spent in the job before things fell apart.

I had eagerly taken on a management position with a new organization, giving up a long-term job I had enjoyed. The problem developed in a few short months: a clashing of personalities between me and my boss, the CEO of the organization. He was a 'Warrior;' I was a 'Nurturer.' He loved hard science; I loved soft skills. He relied on a yelling-bullying modus operandi; I chose to reason and placate. What we had in common was a love of learning and a commitment to working hard. We also had in common a high regard for our reputations. My reputation didn't survive our differences.

I was unknown to my colleagues. They grew wary of me, as they were compelled to choose between their powerful boss and a belittled colleague. Our morning hellos were fraught, before they stopped altogether.

Stressed, humiliated, and depressed, I succumbed to sick leave, then resigned. As I said earlier, the whole sorry episode took only 10 months.

My partner wrapped me in his arms and rebuilt my confidence. My sister and brother-in-law let me drift around their house one weekend, in a fog of depression. Two close friends mopped my face and bolstered me over bacon, eggs, and coffee. My eldest sister invited me into her Wild Women group. These women knew when to ask questions and when to be silent. My lovely twin brother brought me to a bulldog of a lawyer, where I wept my story into the jaws of the legal system. The lawyer's first letter to my workplace quickly brought capitulation and a large cash offer. His second letter earned his fees. I was given a nest egg that carried me through coaching school and through the first years of little income.

Overall, I was lucky. I had people working on my behalf to help me recover some sense of justice, and my self-esteem. I didn't retire, but went on to a new career. The experience, though, gave me a deeply-felt empathy for those I hear from who have gone through similar experiences.

In this chapter, we have the stories of three people who retired for reasons beyond their control. Each story gives us a sense of the devastation of precipitous retirement. Each storyteller shows resilience in adapting to their unexpected retirement, going from depression, outrage, and humiliation to joy, gratitude, and hope.

Articles in this chapter
- *Retirement: Out with a whimper, not a bang*
- *Slapped with a working notice just before retirement*
- *Terminated: My career handed to me in a box*
- *Self-coaching questions*

There was no gold watch or plaque to thank me for my years of service, just a box full of 'work memories' and a wall hanging that said, "she who leaves a trail of glitter will never be forgotten." – Shirley

Retirement: Out with a whimper, not a bang

Jean Murphy
Retired French Immersion Kindergarten Teacher

Overview

Sidelined from a previously delightful teaching career by unrealistic workplace expectations, Jean retired a year before her 'X' factor. From the viewpoint of nine years post-retirement, she tells the tale of her grief, depression, recovery, and new-found happiness.

After many years of 'passion and purpose' teaching French Immersion Kindergarten, I was forced to retire a year early. That is, one year before I had reached my 'X' factor for optimal monthly pension payouts, and a year before my marriage was counting on it. A vocation that had once brought me much, much joy, and for which I was highly respected by administrators, colleagues, students, and parents alike, had by this point turned me into nothing more than a conveyor belt, dumping out numeracy and literacy statistics, rather than nurturing the whole child. I had given my ALL to each student, to the point that, after each parent-teacher interview, and every set of report cards, I felt as though I had just given birth. A brief bout of situational depression eight years prior to my eventual retirement date (which at the time had seemed like a blip on the radar, a "What-the-hell-was-THAT-all-about?" moment) had not prepared me for the debilitating illness that, characterized by ongoing insomnia, general lack of will, and fear of the classroom, sidelined me completely.

Madame fell and bumped her head

Of course, initially, there was grief at having to leave two alternate, all-day classes of wonderful little people without much warning. ("Madame fell and bumped her head.") Not to mention the shame I felt at not being up to the task of changing with the times, keeping up with the unrealistic expectations that had become educational trends by then. I am a concrete sequential Type 'A' person, a person who gets things done efficiently and effectively, so what was the problem? I couldn't have known that it was to take many months of tinkering with meds, rest, counselling, and the loving support of my family to bring me back to the cheerful, confident, fully functional person I once was, and am again today.

Be prepared to sell the prize collection of comics

Teachers in Ontario, if they are fiscally savvy, should not have too many money worries in retirement. We had two cars on the road, no mortgage, and our health. We had attended a couple of retirement workshops, provided by our union, but the biggest takeaway I recall from those sessions was that we might need to be prepared to sell "the prize collection of comics", for example, to make up the difference between our usual take-home pay, and the pension cheque. The word 'gap' was used a lot. Unfortunately, as I was struggling to stay afloat at work, my household had committed to a kitchen renovation that was to go way, WAY beyond the estimated cost. My small retirement gratuity was eaten up by that renovation, leaving me feeling trapped in a house I was beginning to feel we could no longer afford. Additionally, we had built up many wonderful gardens which, at the time, I had no interest in keeping up. Add guilt to the above list of emotions.

In our very sketchy retirement plans, my husband was to retire a year before me. (I had had the good fortune to be at home with our young children, so he had accumulated more years of experience than I.) Instead, we retired at the same time. I very much regret that, after an equally challenging teaching career, he did not have that time to take up new hobbies or throw himself into his current ones, read more books, listen to his music (loudly), watch sci-fi and post-apocalyptic movies, and just be still. Instead, he was forced to become a big part of my recovery.

Fast forward

Fast forward nine years. Our two children are grown, and have happy, meaningful lives of their own. Our daughter is currently teaching French Immersion Kindergarten in a public school in Ontario. I have much respect for what she does, and does well, but part of me still worries about the rigours of the job. More and more, early childhood educators are being required to not just dispense information, but to parent. Our son and his young family are on a three-year posting to Beijing, so if I had had my sights set on being a big part of my grandkids' lives, those plans are currently on hold. Not to mention my worry about the hardships and dangers associated with life in a very polluted, communist country.

So, what does retirement now look like, and is there much to recommend it? Yes, yes, and more yesses. Some new retirees have to learn to say 'No' to the barrage of requests for their time and talent, but that has not been an issue for me, perhaps because of my inauspicious start. Since sleep has often been elusive, and because for my entire career I chose to be at work by 8:00, I now stay in bed unless there is some need to be somewhere at a specific time. What a treat, then, to be able to stay up to watch the news, like a real adult! My general health is good, apart from, thanks to genetics, osteoarthritis. It is hard to explain to a sound person just how much modification can be required for arthritics. Gardening, for example, becomes more and more painful, less and less enjoyable. I am learning to pick and choose my tasks, and the times at which I will do them. Also, my husband has taken on much more of the heavy going, and we are choosing to downsize the area under cultivation.

Music has always been very important to me. During my years at home with children, I took up piano lessons. While I am a terrible sight reader, I love to accompany myself using a basic play-mostly-by-ear approach. Christmas music particularly speaks to me — so what if I begin playing it in October, and don't put it away until May? The desire to play children's songs is a very big impetus now. (I'm currently working on the Bob the Builder theme song...) Some of my closest friendships have been forged through music, particularly in choirs and barbershop quartets. Indeed, one of my best friends passed away recently. Not only do I miss her person, I also miss the song that originally brought us together. During my Kindergarten years, particularly since it was Second Language learning, I used music and song every day, all day, for instructional purposes and community-building. An accomplishment of which I am still proud is the compiling of more than 100 little French songs, many original, in a recording for each child on 'graduation' day.

Moving to music has been hugely important to me in retirement. Obviously, as the arthritis progresses, it is essential to keep moving. I have learned so much, and grown so much since adopting Nia eight years ago on the insistence of other retirees 'of a certain age'. It is a dance practice which incorporates yoga and martial arts, but has a very heavy emphasis on spiritual, mental, and emotional well-being.

While I was teaching full time, I did not have, take, or make the time for fitness. Just getting to 3:30 on a Friday consumed all my energy (mental, emotional, physical, and spiritual), and a typical Friday evening saw me fast asleep in front of the TV after supper and a couple glasses of wine. Not much fun for my husband... One of the greatest, more recent joys of my retirement has been joining the YMCA. We are very lucky in our community to have an amazing, new, well-run facility. It must be stated that my main reason for undertaking a more active lifestyle was and is to get myself, specifically my back, in the best shape I can for a flight to and from Beijing in a few months. To my surprise, as I am a person who doesn't usually even like to get her hair wet except while shampooing, the pool has been the most soothing, yet effective therapy. Even though I'm not a swimmer, I look forward to pain-free splashing about with the little ones.

Thunderstorms and fireflies

While there was no retirement party for me, no sunset dinner cruise on the Chi-Cheemaun ferry in my honour, I did receive many cards and meaningful messages from my closest workmates, family, and friends. One card suggested that the most difficult part about retiring would be knowing when to have your coffee break. This lack of structure posed little problem for me, apart from my not always knowing what day of the week it was. It must now be said, Fridays in the staff room, with special snacks and good-natured bantering, were one of the things I came to miss most when I retired.

I realize today that retirement truly started working for me when I began to look for the small happinesses first: an unusual sunset, the magic and might of a thunderstorm, fireflies where I had never seen them before, the return of the orioles, a brief conversation with someone who needed a walker to approach the pool, but swims like a fish because she was a medalist in synchronized swimming. No need to look for BIG meaning in retirement when, with eyes and heart wide open, the world is out there to help us sort things out.

Perhaps I should get another job, briefly, something like a greeter at Wal-Mart, so I can retire again, properly, as the Hallmark cards say I should...

I realize today that retirement truly started working for me when I began to look for the small happinesses first: an unusual sunset, the magic and might of a thunderstorm, fireflies where I had never seen them before, the return of the orioles... – Jean

Slapped with a working notice just before retirement

By Nancy
Retired Senior Project Manager

Overview

At the age of 50, after 28 years of service with her organization, Nancy was given a 'working notice.' This story tells how she struggled through the long, painful layoff process and the triumph of the new life she created for herself.

Before I got a chance to retire, I was laid off. It all happened within a week. As many of us were teleworkers, we received notices in our electronic calendars of a 30-minute face-to-face meeting. No phone call, no email, no preamble. Just a swirl of rumours.

At the meeting, after a very brief *blah blah blah* from the director, he left the room. The Human Resources representative read the letter of termination. My termination date was set 18 months from that day! WHAT!!! I could no longer listen to the HR rep talk about outsourced help, pension, the employee stock ownership plan, etc. I thought: A year and a half from now! And you expect me to perform my duties professionally? To be respectful of my director and his superiors? To meet with my peers and project team like nothing has happened? Are you nuts!

Working notices

This layoff process is called a 'working notice'. With a working notice, you have time to find another job elsewhere before you leave. With a working notice, the company doesn't have to pay a big severance package because, literally, the company has given you notice.

Staggering forward

Realizing that I no longer wanted to work as a project manager of high-pressure, high-exposure projects, I took advantage of the outsourced help: I took tests to determine what I want, what I'm good at, and what kind of work to avoid. I learned about resume writing; I had not created a resume in 20 years! I did some therapy. Am I not good enough? How unfair to be let go after 28 years! How was I to make a living now? Should I retire or find work? I also had a major financial challenge to face: my leukemia pills cost $5,700 per month. My company's insurance used to pay completely.

So, this was the start of my long, painful termination. Working notices may be good for companies, they may even be good for some employees. For me, it was very difficult, stressful, and unnerving. I had given this company all that I could give, working long hours, often through weekends and during my vacations. Twenty-eight years of unstinting service, 50 years old, 5 years from full-pension retirement, 18 months notice. Now what?

Fighting mad

They say you go through the phases of mourning when you're laid off. I believe it. I mourned the pride in my work, my dedication, my self-worth, and my self-confidence.

And I was so angry! So angry! I'd worked diligently for 28 years. I had even helped them plan downsizing in previous years! As a manager, I had had to lay off some of my own people. I knew that meant finding the people who were the weakest links. Now facing being laid off myself, I questioned why I was considered a weak link. What had I failed to do in my work? And I was only five years from fully-paid retirement. I'd been dreaming about it for so long.

Although I refrained from making disparaging remarks to anyone at the office, I brought plenty home to my husband.

Panic

The real kicker was that I couldn't afford my $5,700 per month leukemia pills. I need to pay them until I'm 65, when OHIP picks up the slack. My company offered to transfer my insurance coverage from an employee plan to an independent plan. Because of the leukemia, however, that insurance company didn't want me. After researching insurance coverages with other companies, I discovered that none wanted me. I was panicking! Then, good news: my husband George checked with his company's insurance. He was told that it would pay the full amount. Yay!

What we didn't know at the time was that George's boss was negotiating with another insurance company in order to lower insurance costs, starting in the new year. This new insurance company paid only $10,000 per year for meds, rather than the $90,000 coverage I had received from the previous company. That wouldn't even cover two months of pills!!! The situation was making me crazy! What could I do now? I had heard many years ago about the Trillium Foundation, but I never thought it was for me. Still, I did some research and learned that it could take me on. Phew! I could breathe again! Because of the slow process of all the confirmation letters and red tape, I ended up paying $20,000 before I started to see reimbursements from Trillium. Yikes! I was accumulating travel points on my Mastercard, for sure!

Cut adrift

I was managing a few projects when I received my letter of termination. As the weeks and months progressed, one by one I completed these projects. During the many years I was project manager, I was given new projects as soon as, or even before, projects were completed. Now, none were given to me, or to my seven colleagues. I worried at my desk, waiting for emails or phone calls assigning new projects. None came.

During that 18-month period, my manager was assigned to another department. The new manager never called to introduce himself; he never invited me to group meetings. A few months after his appointment, he was replaced by another manager. Again, no news. I found out about these changes through the company's phone book. It turned into an absurd game, figuring out who was my boss each week.

Acceptance

After months of unrelenting confusion, low self-esteem, and mourning, I started to realize that I could not influence the executive decision to shelve me until my termination date. The decision was motivated only by money-saving and organizational restructuring — nothing personal. Once I fully realized this, and owned it, I started to think outside of myself, beyond my desk, my home, and my despair. Finally, I started my healing... towards a more positive energy... towards the possibility of smiling again.

Making a life

Months before my termination date, George and I met our financial advisor to acquire and discuss our long-term financial forecast. The first thing he said when we sat down with him at Tim Horton's was, "You can retire if you want to." I felt I could breathe again; the grey cloud over my head had been blown away. The very conservative numbers he showed us proved his statement. George would continue to work for a couple of years more, as we had planned. I now felt I had a choice: if I wanted to work, it would be because I chose to work. What a feeling!

I always wanted to volunteer, but working full time had limited my choices. When I retired, I continued to volunteer at the Library To Go program, bringing bags of books, music, and DVDs to people who can no longer visit the library. I continued to volunteer for an organization that provides therapeutic horseback riding for physically challenged people. I also continued to enjoy my role as Event Coordinator on the Board of Directors for a local trail club.

To my volunteer portfolio I have now added one-on-one weekly visits to six residents at a long-term care home. The amateur theatre group is also a new volunteer opportunity for me. Actually, even though I work for no pay at the theatre, I don't consider myself a volunteer. It is so fun!

Sailing the world

George and I own a Jeanneau 37-foot sailboat, which we keep in a small harbour town nearby. We have been planning, learning about, and experiencing cruising for many years now. Soon, we will start cruising every six months — for six months at a time — until we can no longer enjoy it. Whenever we end our six-month stretch, we will store the boat wherever we are and return to Canada. We plan to start by sailing the Caribbean and British Virgin Islands for two to three years, then cross over to the Mediterranean. After a couple of years there and in Europe, we'll sail back toward the Americas, where we will sail along the East Coast of South America and then back north along its western coast. Exciting!

Photo: Nancy

Lessons Learned in Retirement

A few lessons learned

We keep learning as we move through the years and through the various phases of our lives. This whole experience of ending my career and starting a new phase taught me a few lessons. One is to plan for the future, but to trust my capabilities when storms threaten. Also, if I were to work for a business again, I would never give up vacation time and evenings with my family in order to complete a business deliverable. And, finally, I've learned the value of creating a peaceful harbour for myself in the world. There is nothing quite like coming through a life storm safely, to a place of acceptance and contentment. I am pleased to say I have accomplished this.

Working notices may be good for companies, they may even be good for some employees. For me, it was very difficult, stressful, and unnerving. I had given this company all that I could give, working long hours, often through weekends and during my vacations. Twenty-eight years of unstinting service, 50 years old, 5 years from full-pension retirement, 18 months notice. Now what? – Nancy

Terminated: My career handed to me in a box

By Barb Carriere
Retired Manager – Continuing Education

> ## Overview
> *Barb describes her journey from the crushing experience of sudden job termination to a state of acceptance and gratitude.*

"Your position has been deemed redundant." The following words were a blur. I felt as if I had just smashed head first into a brick wall.

The shock of the unexpected termination of my long-term employment was shattering to my physical, emotional, and mental well-being. The following two weeks were filled with tears, anger, and numerous conversations with those who offered their ear and their support. A Career Coach Service was available as part of the severance package and I found it provided an opportunity to understand the phases of change and the importance of caring for yourself, as well as giving me a chance to look into the future and set goals. What I found most helpful was the coach's positive support of the person I was, outside of the 'job.'

Who am I?

As the fog lifted, I realized I was grieving not only the loss of my job, but the loss of my identity. For many of us, our families, community members, and friends identify us by our job title and the work we do each day. When that job no longer exists, the question "who am I?" looms large. I've heard that losing a job ranks among the top five life situations that cause the most stress in our lives. Feelings of shock, numbness, anger, and frustration are normal and recognizing this assisted me in committing to move forward.

Prior to my job loss, my husband and I had listed for sale the home we had built eight years previously. A decision to downsize both property and home felt right at that point in our lives. Looking back, I realize this served as a positive distraction for me during the healing process, as it helped me to focus on the future. I began creating a photo book of memories of our home, which brought many smiles on those sad days.

At the two-week point, I was able to return to my office, at a time when few staff members were present, to clean out my personal belongings. A sense of closure sustained me as I walked out of the building with my career in a box and confirmation that I was no longer an employee.

What helped me in the following days was a truly wonderful gift, a gift that reminds me each day of how others saw me in my work. It was a 'word cloud' presented to me at a 'Remember When' party, created from feedback I received from fellow employees. It is a continual reminder of those attributes I have that cannot be taken away by a job termination.

Getting grounded again

I found that, wherever I was, questions about my job loss were plentiful. I developed a truthful, brief, and positive response to the questions, which flowed more easily the more times I delivered it.

As I moved towards acceptance of my situation, I took the opportunity to give to others and to volunteer my time as I had in the past. Giving back to the community felt good and reminded me about the positive actions that occur each day in our world.

Hiking, walking, snowshoeing, and yoga allowed me to maintain and expand my physical well-being and provided a time for quiet reflection. The gift of time provided the privilege of becoming more actively involved with my grandchildren, creating new memories. The impetus to reconnect with old friends and acquaintances took on a new level of importance. My life had been so busy when I was working that I had let important relationships slide and was in danger of losing touch. Now was the time to rebuild those connections. These 'dates' provided support and laughter as we reminisced about old times and caught up on the here and now.

I spent peaceful time each day in the crisp outdoors, reflecting on my path ahead. It became obvious that I already had multiple identities in my current relationships as wife, mother, grandmother, friend, sister, and neighbour. Within these roles I searched for my passions and examined how best to fulfill them.

At week six, I picked up the phone and called to enquire about possible work at a nearby garden centre, one I've visited rather regularly since we built our home. My love of gardening led me to accept the offer of part-time work in early April. Working in a warm greenhouse with my hands in the soil, meeting coworkers, and learning new skills provided an exciting new focus for me.

Right under our noses

Then our realtor called. The words "we've got a deal" hit me hard; I felt both happy and sad knowing that the weeks ahead would be filled with packing and the search for a new home. Unsure of where our new home would actually be, we started investigating a number of towns within a two-hour radius. Another force in our life was pushing me forward towards new pathways. Spring was in the air with a sense of a fresh start. Crocuses and trilliums were sprouting and the excitement of challenges lay ahead.

We were two weeks away from possession date and, through all our travels, had not found a new town or a new home. We started working on Plan B, in case we ran out of time. Then, one day, I walked through the door of a house in a wonderful neighbourhood and I knew I had found our new home. It was just across the bay from the home we sold; for all our searching, we ended up within minutes of the same town. Sometimes we don't see that what we really need has been right in front of us all the time.

Letting others in

During these difficult times, I learned to allow others 'in' to support me. I recognized that my sadness was lightened when others helped me carry it. One afternoon the phone rang and my sister said, "I've lost my job too — they've declared bankruptcy!" All of a sudden, the roles switched and I was providing the shoulder to cry on and the ear to listen. Even though my wounds were still fresh, they were healing well enough that I could now support her. How life delivers messages through mysterious ways. "Everything happens at the right time and in the right place" became the mantra that carried me through those early, cloudy days, and still provides a framework when reviewing daily events.

I see that the dramatic event of job loss provided me with the opportunity to design each day, to recognize that each day is a gift, and to become aware that I have so very much for which to be grateful.

So along comes the cloud and according to well-known lore, it also comes with the thing call the Silver Lining, something no one ever thinks about initially — sort of like insurance or boot liners. – Rose

Self-Coaching Questions

It is not in the stars to hold our destiny but in ourselves. – William Shakespeare

Dealing with Unexpected Retirement

- What are you doing to protect your health?
- What can you do to control your exit from the workforce?
- What planning might help you adjust better in the event of an unexpected early retirement?
- What action can you take now?

Following Frank into retirement: 5 months to go

Frank in a nutshell

I am a 58-year-old unambitious overachiever. I have worked hard at several jobs in research and manufacturing, none of which has been boring, but that for the most part have left me personally unsatisfied. I am pretty frustrated now in my current position. In the past I would have moved on to another company many years ago, but my partner, Suzanne, and I do not want to relocate again. If I were passionate about my work, I would consider consulting, however instead I find myself pondering the leap into retirement. I've been asked to share in this newsletter my pinball decision path towards retirement and over the next several months I will be writing about the many arguments I've had with myself and the "Ah-ha" moments that have helped me make my decision. I have given notice to my employer and will be retiring at the end of the year.

The struggle of work, family, and my own priorities

I have enjoyed a successful career and my work has provided a good living for Suzanne and me, and our three children (now all in their twenties and almost living on their own). In my early 40s I decided that the jump to senior management required more personal commitment to the job than I was willing to offer. My priorities in life have remained family-first, work-second, and Frank-third. As work demanded more and more of my energy, I let my personal interests and activities fall by the wayside to ensure that my family life was relatively unaffected. Eventually our lifestyle was dominated by my work and we decided to follow our priorities and make one last move based on our vision of our future life. We selected an area in which we could envisage retiring and decided to bear the consequences of the poor employment prospects. We felt that if we made the move many years in advance of retirement we would have a good chance to settle into the area rather than have a radical shift upon retirement.

Suzanne, after 13 years as an at-home mother, rejoined the workforce to provide us with a safety net until I was once again gainfully employed. I eventually joined a company that allowed me to work from a home office but that required considerable travel in Ontario and Quebec. While Suzanne and I provided a stable home base for our children to progress from public through high schools, we both are growing increasingly intolerant of our situations in our respective jobs and are ready for a change.

Retirement decision factors

In a way we are fortunate in that I have changed jobs too frequently to be tied to a company pension plan and don't need to wait for any "magic" combinations of age and years of service. Our kids will be finished post secondary schooling next spring. Suzanne is retiring two months earlier than me and, since we're best mates and do most things together, her upcoming retirement was a major factor in my decision. We have lived for the past 11 years in an area and house in which we intend to stay for as long as we are physically able. We will be relying primarily on our RSP and other savings, but should have enough for a 2-week trip abroad each year as well as some tooling around North America. I've done a detailed cash flow that incorporates all our possible income, an inflation rate of 2%, a return on investment of 4% and any large expenses that we can anticipate in the next 40 years. It has helped us make our decision, but there is really no way to know how life will turn out.

Anything is possible in retirement

As I mentioned earlier, I used to enjoy many activities and I'm looking forward to rediscovering as many of them as I can and having the time to pursue new ones. Anything is possible in retirement — accepting an overseas post for a couple of years to allow us to explore a new country; reading up on subjects that have always interested me; taking better care of my body by being more active and doing yoga. Now that I've made my decision, I can't wait.

2 Creating a New Identity

Shortly after taking maternity leave from IBM, I attended a party of business people. I was asked by a young man what I did for a living. I told him I was a stay-at-home mother. The man's eyes lost focus, then quickly scanned the room for refuge in some more worthy creature. Anyone would be more interesting! I was shocked at how quickly I had gone from being relevant to being stereotyped as a has-been who no longer had value.

Retirement can leave us feeling that way. When we enter retirement, we leave behind our identity as it was in our careers — labelled, measured, respected, and rewarded by the external world. We risk being stereotyped as feeble, forgetful, stubborn, and helpless.

My friend and coaching colleague Lynne Maukonen has three particularly good thoughts about identity in retirement:

1. *Focusing on whatever you truly want and fully engaging in that — not caring what others think — is an excellent way to keep from the sense of being 'less than,' a feeling that can so easily pop up unbidden.*

2. *An important perspective to adopt is that you are retiring to something and not just from something. And make your new focus who you want to be more than what you want to be.*

3. *If we view retirement less like an end and more like a transition or even a series of transitions, the adjustment will likely be much smoother. Cohen and Schlossberg (2004) have compared retirees to students who come to college — some knowing what they want to do and others not yet knowing. So, they use the first year at college as an opportunity to expose themselves to new things. Retirees can choose to approach retirement in the same way, as a liberating time of exploration."*

Whatever identity we build for ourselves in retirement, the aim is that it will reward us with great personal satisfaction. We can let go of the work world's success-yardsticks, which measure size of salary, titles, promotions, number of publications, performance appraisals, billing rate, hours billed, overtime worked, size of investment portfolio, types of cars, amount spent on vacations, and years of employment. Instead, we can focus on our own measures and understanding what fulfills us.

In this chapter you'll hear from a guy who wants to recreate himself in retirement after 37½ years as a dentist. Another person likens retirement to a small death, the death of our work identity. He discusses retirement in terms of mortality, vanity, and reincarnation. A third article cheers us on to claim our power in spite of our wrinkles. And, finally, you can check out 16 questions to help clarify who you want to be in retirement. The chapter ends with some self-coaching questions.

Articles in this chapter:

- *Will my identity retire with me?*
- *Retirement — la petite mort*
- *In praise of wattles and wrinkles*
- *Still don't know what you want to be when you grow up?*
- *Self-coaching questions*

My 'hairy eyeball', once an effective deterrent to a bad idea or a poorly chosen comment from staff, has lost its former authority. – Phil

Will my identity retire with me?

By Phil McCavity
Soon-To-Be-Retired Dentist

Overview

Having been a dentist for the past 37½ years, "Dr. McCavity" explores what that will mean to his identity in retirement.

As part of my retirement plan, and after a hiatus of five years, I have rejoined the pipe band with which I used to play. Last night at practice, I had a chat with two fellow pipers about retirement. Jack, 78, retired from Ontario Hydro about 24 years ago. Ian is a judge and will have to retire next year when he turns 75. We were discussing how some people view a large part of themselves in terms of their job or career and how retirement means that you are, in effect, no longer "Justice Smith" or "Dr. Jones". Some people struggle with this.

Just another white-haired retired guy

I am 60 and about to semi-retire. A nice young fellow takes over my dental practice in January and I will be staying on part-time for six months. Then I will be fully retired and, although I will always have my degree, I will in effect no longer be "Dr. McCavity". I will, instead, just be another white-haired retired guy. Or, as my kids see it, an OLD retired guy. Will this be a difficult transition? Do I self-identify as "Dr. McCavity"? Well, I could count on one hand the number of times I have introduced myself to anyone, patients included, as "Dr. McCavity". I don't wear scrubs or a lab coat at work. I don't go looking to be recognized in the community in which I live and practice as anyone other than just another citizen.

Turning off Dr. McCavity

And yet, I have been "Dr. McCavity" for the past 37½ years; I suspect that identity is deep within me. When I walk away from my career in a little over six months, will I be able to turn off the dentist persona like turning off a switch? Will it bother me to not go into the office and be Dr. McCavity; to not be able to get people out of pain; to not receive thanks for doing a procedure painlessly; to not be able to do something that allows someone to smile again?

"What do you do for a living?" ... "I'm a dentist" ...will become ... "I'm retired."

Right now this sounds very appealing. There are a lot of things I intend to turn my attention to in retirement. I've had enough of being a dentist, and I am looking forward to change and reinventing my life as just plain Phil McCavity. I think.

It has now been a little over seven months since I sold my practice and semi-retired, and about seven weeks since I fully retired. I have not missed any aspect of work for even a nanosecond. – Phil

Lessons Learned in Retirement

Retirement — *la petite mort*

By Anson Laytner
Retired Interreligious Initiative Program Manager,
School of Theology & Ministry, Seattle University

Overview

No longer essential at a workplace where he once played an integral role, Anson describes the insight that transition gave him.

The French call an orgasm *la petite mort* but, as much as I like orgasms, I think *la petite mort* ought to refer to retirement.

You see, the other week I had an opportunity to visit my old workplace. It made me feel like I had died and come back as a ghost.

The buildings looked the same; I recognized familiar faces among the students, faculty and staff. But I was struck by the fact that everything was going along just fine without my presence and participation.

The program I used to manage was now being run by someone else; the relationships I had cultivated now were being nurtured by another person; the alliances I had forged now involved other people. Life and work flowed on without me.

In truth, it was as if I had died, gone to heaven, and returned to earth for a quick visit. Initially, it was very disconcerting — and depressing — to feel so unessential in a place where I once had played such an integral role.

Reincarnation

Retirement gave me an intimation of my mortality. Going back to my old workplace was a blow to my ego, but it also helped me put my life, and my life's work, into a better perspective. As the song says: "All we are is dust in the wind..." or as Kohelet (Ecclesiastes) put it: "Vanity of vanities! All is vanity! What real value is there for a person in all the labor that he does beneath the sun?"

Actually, this is not a depressing thought but a corrective, even inspirational, one. All too often while we are working, we yearn for more time for ourselves or to be with our loved ones; time to focus on what really matters in life. "If only I had more time," is the mantra of the working person. Now, in retirement, we have that time.

Unlike death, retirement, *la petite mort,* affords us the time and opportunity to resurrect or reincarnate ourselves as often as we care to, so that we can add significance and meaning to our days.

So I continue to ask myself "How am I going to spend my remaining time on this planet?"

— **❝** —————————————————————————

Unlike death, retirement, la petite mort, affords us the time and opportunity to resurrect or reincarnate ourselves as often as we care to, so that we can add significance and meaning to our days. – Anson

—————————————————————————— **❞** —

In praise of wattles and wrinkles

By Mariella Hoy

Overview

At this stage of life, we have immense power and influence, despite our gnarly appearance.

When I started going to the gym again, after being away for a dozen years, being in a communal change room once more reminded me that my body had changed in the interim. I was about to add 'not for the better,' but I'm trying out a new way of thinking: our bodies change constantly throughout our lives and the changes are natural and, yes, even beautiful. I'm thinking of old trees, and how gorgeous their gnarly bits can be.

The Angel Oak

Take the Angel Oak Tree of Charleston, South Carolina. When I saw a photograph of that tree I thought 'intricate,' 'complex,' 'a host to other life,' and 'magnificent.'

According to Wikipedia...

> *The Angel Oak a Southern live oak (Quercus virginiana) located in Angel Oak Park on Johns Island near Charleston, South Carolina. Angel Oak is 400 years old. It stands 66.5 ft (20 m) tall, measures 28 ft (8.5 m) in circumference, and produces shade that covers 17,200 square feet (1,600 m²). Its longest branch distance is 187 ft in length.[1]*

As I was reading various descriptions about this tree, it occurred to me that you could describe people of retirement age in almost identical terms. Both the Angel Oak and retirees...

- provide shelter from storms;
- sustain a giant network;
- have evolved to withstand forceful winds;
- do not need height to astound; and
- are known for their majestic canopy, rather than their stature.

---

1 Angel Oak. (2022, August 8). In Wikipedia. https://en.wikipedia.org/wiki/Angel_Oak

My mother in the mirror

That is not to say that seeing the aging of my body is not shocking at times. My first day in the gym change room, I saw myself in the mirror and standing beside me was a beautiful, young woman who was wearing a matched set of lacy, apricot underwear. No extra flesh, wrinkles, or droopiness marred her exquisiteness. Comparing myself to her, I imagined I was my mother peering at us from the mirror.

I could almost see the wattles forming under my chin, those loose folds of flesh that old people dangle, like the dewlap on a moose.

Yet, I love the unloveliness of the Angel Oak. It's the gnarliness, the agedness, the unloveliness that makes it so beautiful. I don't look for flaws. I say, "Wow, that is fantastic! I should go visit that tree."

Embracing crepe bosoms

Why are we so hard on ourselves? So what if we develop spots, wattles, and wrinkles as we age? Let's find the character and beauty in cauliflower ears and drooping noses. Bravo to skinny-shanked men and crepe-bosomed women.

Some of the most powerful photos I've seen have been black and white images of old people — ancient souls with their life experiences etched in their flesh and radiating through their eyes. No dyed hair. No makeup. Just them — straight up. The essence of their lives grooved into their faces.

The state of our exterior cladding isn't important at this age. Cuteness may be what kept our parents from disowning us when we were babies, through colic and tantrums. Beauty may have mattered when we were young adults, seeking out mates. And we needed to be physically strong during the middle years working or raising children. Now we are past all that. Sure, we need to be physically healthy, but cuteness, beauty, and peak physical strength aren't as necessary.

Rising to the challenge

What does matter, then? I read recently that we have within us many hidden gems, and that life is about uncovering these gems, giving them to the world. Or maybe what matters is rising to the challenge. At the gym, I regularly see a man and his partner taking a yoga class at 6:30 in the morning. He comes to support his partner as she strengthens her body so she can tolerate her cancer treatments. And then he heads off to work. A 95-year-old woman recently told her gym friends that she wouldn't be able to get to the pool as early as usual... because she had to get to her line dancing class. I met a woman who has swum at the gym pool regularly since 1976.

She taught swim classes for years. Now, due to severe arthritis, she uses two walking sticks to get about. But she is always cheerful. These older people are exhibiting admirable inner resources in circumstances that might level younger individuals.

Claiming our power

Maybe at this stage of life it is time to see and to claim our power. Like the massive oak tree, we too have broad reach and extensive networks. We have built a base of knowledge through experience and learned important lessons. We can sow our acorns with confidence. Our immense canopies can be used to protect and nurture the seedlings we care about.

I haven't yet learned to see myself this way, but perhaps it's time to step back and to really look in the mirror — to acknowledge that I am now my mother. Just as my changing exterior periodically surprises me, so too does the changing of my life stage. And with this new life stage — if I'd only admit it to myself — comes significant power and influence... and the responsibility to use them well.

And why not think kindlier of myself and others my age, even if we have wattles and wrinkles? When I'm changing at the gym next time, I'm going to make a point of admiring my fellow oaks, looking past their outer cladding, to see their power. And as my sister said, we need to take seriously what the generation before us has to illuminate, that we should "ask upward." Only imagine what they have to offer us.

Just as my changing exterior periodically surprises me, so too does the changing of my life stage. And with this new life stage — if I'd only admit it to myself — comes significant power and influence... and the responsibility to use them well.

– Mariella

Still don't know what you want to be when you grow up?

By Mariella Hoy

Overview

No longer defined by our work, retirement gives us another chance to figure out who we want to be and what we want out of life.

When we were young, people would ask "What do you want to be when you grow up?" Most of us thought up an acceptable answer: firefighter, astronaut, teacher, doctor. Then we spent half a lifetime building and inhabiting different careers, wearing different hats. And now retirement is pending, or upon us, and we still may not know what we really want to be when we grow up.

And it can be unsettling.

In retirement, like children again, we are free to choose. Our options are wide open. We can be exactly what we want to be.

Reframing the question

Only this time, it's not a career that drives the choice and, unlike children, we are not presented with a list of acceptable options. No longer defined by our work, how do we answer that question: What do you want to be when you grow up?

Maybe the question needs to be reframed. Maybe the question should be "Who do you want to be when you grow up?" It's still a big question, but it now underscores the point that we are no longer defined — or confined — by our work and can become whomever we want and do whatever turns our cranks.

A rare opportunity

Retirement gives us a rare chance to really figure out what we want out of life. When I was a kid, I wanted to be a ballerina, a priest (they had more power than nuns), and a detective. Today, I sometimes do ballet balance moves at the gym; the desire to be a priest has vanished; and detection is a tool I use when working with people who are planning their retirements. I don't know how much time I still have on this good, green earth, but I hope to have enough time to try many new things. What, I don't yet know! I want to continue to play with my camera and to write. I want to be peaceful, ready to laugh, and adaptable to change.

What about you? As a kid, what did you want to be when you grew up? And now, who do you want to be in retirement? What will make your retirement terrific?

In the *Self-coaching questions* section, below, is a list of 16 questions to trigger some ideas for you. I hope you find it helpful in determining who you want to be in retirement. Good luck.

— 66 ——————————————————————

The dreams come easily now. – Joan

—————————————————————— 99 —

❓ Self-Coaching Questions

When I was young, I admired clever people. Now that I am old, I admire kind people." – Abraham Joshua Heschel

Creating a New Identity

16 questions to help figure it out!

I've put together a list of questions that will help you clarify who you want to be in retirement.

1. If you were to wander through your home looking at the things (and people) you've put into your life, what do they tell you about yourself?
2. What do your old report cards reveal: Any gems in the comments from your teachers? In which subjects did you excel? Which subjects did you enjoy?
3. When have you lost track of time because you were so absorbed in something?
4. What do you want to get better and better at doing?
5. What kinds of things do people come to you for help with (what are you known for)?
6. What motivates you in relation to retirement — for example, happy relationships, money worries, helping others, the next generations, your creativity, finding pleasure and contentment, creating a legacy, adventuring, being productive?
7. How do you define success as it relates to your retirement?
8. When in your life have you felt completely comfortable in your own skin?
9. If you were to leaf through a file folder of all the dream jobs you ever wanted (or had), what would they tell you about your dreams/about yourself?
10. What in this world drives you crazy enough that you would help to fix it — for example, a product, a system, a falsehood, or a practice?
11. What has been a consistent thread throughout your life?
12. How are you different from everyone else... in your weirdness, your beliefs, your character traits, and the knowledge and skills you've developed?
13. What have been the proudest moments in your life?
14. What did you love about work that you'd like to bring into your retirement?
15. What is one thing you would relish doing for the next 15 to 40 years of your life?
16. In this next phase of your life, what do you want? What do you really want?

Following Frank into retirement:
4 months to go

Hanging up the skates — flip flopping towards retirement

I can just hear the colour commentator in the booth chattering: "I can't see why he's quitting the game when he's at the peak of his career!" My colleagues don't understand my decision. In fact, I'm beginning to dread the question about what I'm going to do next and the subsequent disbelief that I am not going to continue on in my work. Not because it may lessen my standing in their eyes, but because it unfailingly triggers an internal struggle with my ego, my work ethic, and, of course, with my fondness for money. I'll try to explain...

The voices in my head

Over my career, I have built up an impressive C.V. of academic qualifications and industry positions, as well as a reputation as being a diplomatic "straight-shooter." I have always worked hard and, together with my partner Suzanne, we are finally earning enough to have lots of spending money. My ego says, "Damn! I'm good! I shouldn't quit, I should get a new position where I can really make a difference." My work ethic chimes in with: "What do you mean, not working? You're not being a productive member of society. You're not going to be able to help out your children. You should work until you are unable to continue." And, last but not least, Mr. Money slinks in and whispers unctuously, "Wouldn't it be nice to be able to afford that extra holiday, the new appliances, the back-up generator and all those luxuries you've gotten used to just going out and buying?" Or if he's in a meaner mood: "The markets will plunge, CPP and OAS will run dry, and you and Suzanne will be destitute." All of this angst just because I want to stop working for pay!

This trio of voices has caused me months of night sweats. Due to my indecisive state of mind, I've done spreadsheet calculations for retirement for every age from 55 to 65. Retiring at 55 would have given me lots of time to experience this wide world, but retiring at 65 would allow us to buy anything we want and still have lots left over for our kids. I want us to have enough money to be comfortable, but I don't want to work until I'm 65 (or, for that matter, 59).

Quieting the voices

I'm getting pretty good at sending Mr. Money packing with some solid planning and simplifying of our lifestyle to accommodate our budget. My work ethic is tougher to handle, but as I've pointed out to myself many times, once retired, I may not be working for money, but I will have time to be more active in our community. I'll also be available to help out our children with their renovations, dogsitting, and babysitting (if they ever, ever decide to have children themselves). That just leaves my insidious ego buzzing around in my head. It is not really something against which I can use logic. I feel as though I am turning my back on a lifetime of learning and experience, on a way of life. My work is closely intertwined with my identity.

Stumped

So, how do I just let go of something that has occupied about 50% of my waking life? Let me know if you have any good suggestions because I'm stumped. In the face of such staunch opposition from my ego, I'm just shouting it down. I am not in love with my job! It does not define who I really am! I am more than my career! It's been good, but it's over!

In the end it will be up to me to find worth in whatever I choose to do. Once again, I will have to trust in my own judgement, trust that I am making the right move. Forgetting itself, my ego adds: "Well you've certainly shown good judgement throughout your career and life; why should that change now?"

I can just hear the colour commentator in the booth chattering: "I can't see why he's quitting the game when he's at the peak of his career!" – Frank

3 **Rebuilding Routines**

If you haven't yet retired, do you find yourself lost in dreams of what retirement will be like? Do you envision spending six weeks in a far-flung country with your camera and a guidebook for company? Or lying on the couch reading a book from dawn to dusk?

I've discovered that this period of sweet anticipation can change to near panic once retirement is upon us. One person told me they attended a retirement workshop in which they were asked to fill in a calendar for the first three months of retirement and how this big, blank calendar stared back pitilessly. Another said they returned from their first big vacation after retiring and were smacked with the question: Now what? A newly retired friend said that, once the golfing season ended, he could see winter closing in and couldn't imagine what he would do until spring.

With retirement, the weight of responsibility to create the blissful retirement we imagined for years descends upon our shoulders. Yet, our days suddenly have no rigour, no structure, no scaffolding. This lack of routine can send us spinning, like a boat without a rudder. Inertia can engulf us in depression.

In this chapter, you'll hear from newly retired people who experienced the transition from anticipation of infinite possibilities and the riches of limitless time to the shock of being solely responsible for guiding their lives. You'll hear from a nurse, full of anticipation, on her last day of work. A retired teacher tells us about her struggle to create a new definition of success, one that balances productivity with complete absorption in the creative moment. We'll look at how we can find the sweet spot between rigid, over-achieving routines and drifting idleness. Finally, you'll hear from an active, busy person who, after 35 years of work, feels restless in retirement if faced with too much free time.

Articles in this chapter:
- *My last day of work... ever*
- *Of lists and blank pages*
- *Inertia in retirement*
- *Freedom sixty-one*
- *Self-coaching questions*

My last day of work... ever

By Josette Vigneux
Retired Registered Nurse

Overview

Before setting up new routines and structures in retirement, Josette paused to reflect upon and celebrate her 30-year nursing career.

Today was my last day of work... ever. After 30 years I signed in for the last time. It was the last time for so many things, and the start of my next chapter.

My alarm went off at 6:30 a.m. as usual, although I was already up with the dogs at 5:45. I fed them, then grabbed my coffee and went back to bed to savour it while I fully woke up.

Once up, I quickly flipped into my usual routine — I put my steel cut oats into the microwave, put an egg on to boil, got dressed, and did my hair and makeup. I put on a new T-shirt, one that I had found months ago, which had the words "Best Day Ever" boldly across the front. Although I truly love my job, and leave it with mixed emotions, I could not resist this shirt.

On the drive to the hospital, I was excited... but also melancholy. I have spent so much of my life with the people in that building — the nurses, doctors, support staff, patients and their

Photo: Rachal Bullock.

families, cleaners, kitchen staff, and so many more. We are a community and a family. I kind of feel like I am leaving the nest. Scary and exciting at the same time.

The last time

Today was the last time for so many things:

- Last time to try to find that perfect parking spot close to the door
- Last time to take the elevator to the 14th floor (as usual, it took forever coming)
- Last time to open up my computer, print out a new patient list for the day, lead rounds, and tackle whatever else would be thrown my way

- Last time to calm an angry family when things weren't going the way they should, or at least the way they thought they should
- Last time to hear a patient say I had made a difference to their stay in hospital
- Last time to say "Goodnight. See everyone tomorrow!"

Over my 30 years as a nurse, I did so many things. What a wonderful career. The 12-hour shifts were great... when I was younger. I found the Monday-to-Friday 8-hour shifts more suited to me as I 'matured.' I worked in several different areas of the hospital, so I never felt stuck in the same job. I was a staff nurse on the 'Willie Ward.' Urology, officially. This position provided non-stop material for dinner party stories — much to the dismay of the non-medical guests. As co-ordinator of a hip and knee replacement unit, I was proud that we got the place running like an efficient assembly line. For a while, I worked in the Bladder Care Centre. Patients came in for bladder testing — terrified — and left saying, "That wasn't so bad!" My final position, as leader of a medical unit, was by far my most rewarding position. Not only did I work with the nurses and patients, but I also helped the medical students who were learning to become doctors.

Ice cream treats

It is hard to arrange any sort of get-together while at work, because we still have to be available to our patients and their families. But food usually does the trick. In the morning, I spread the word that there would be ice cream treats on the Unit at 2 p.m., after my last set of rounds. Those who could make it showed up. I handed around ice cream sandwiches and popsicles that I had brought, and we had a good visit.

I had only one episode of tears — that with a long-term colleague who came to see me in the morning to say goodbye — but I generally held it together, much to my surprise. I don't actually feel sad about leaving, because I am so excited about what is to come next. We'll see how I do at my retirement party later in the spring, though.

Breaking free

I thought I would leave a little early on my last day, but, as luck would have it, I got busy and ran late. Once done, however, I gathered up the flowers and gifts that people had so generously brought for me. I put on my coat, and said a big goodbye to the medical team members who were doing their end-of-day rounds in the area outside my office. I left my key for the person covering me next week and headed to the elevator for the last time. As I was walking through the lobby towards the door, the retirement balloon that had been given to me broke free from its string and sailed up to the ceiling. I took that as a sign... the sky is the limit!

As I was driving home listening to CBC, I was thinking of that glass of bubbly I would be having to celebrate. So many people were surprised to hear I was retiring. Some said I was too young (I love those people) and some said what will we do without you? (I love them equally.)

My next chapter

Well. I am home now. Bubbly in hand. Toasting with a few close friends.

Today is the first day of my next chapter. I am excited to see how things will unfold as the pages turn. One thing for sure — I will be having coffee in bed tomorrow, with my dogs snuggled next to me.

I think it is important for me to keep an open mind about retirement expectations and "go with the flow" until either our life has developed a pattern or we live happily in chaos.
– Frank

Of lists and blank pages

By Rose Morley
Retired Elementary School Teacher

Overview

Rose discusses the need to find the balance between "necessary routines and the delicious lapse into flow."

Here is the noble, romantic, idealistic view: each day of your retirement is a fresh, clean page upon which you can make your mark, any sort of mark. It is the idea that kept you going while you were longing for retirement. You would catch yourself at any moment of the workday, lived a thousand times before. Ah, here it is, the freedom and unfettered nature of your day. Countless possibilities for what it will look like: a cool drink in the middle of a warm, sunny afternoon with a book on your lap; a clear crisp morning standing on a train platform in a country you have never been to before; the freshness of the morning dew, coffee mug in hand and no watch on your wrist.

The gift (and torment) of the blank page

To regard the days of one's retirement as clean, new sheets of paper is so necessary in order to create the rest of your life. The release of energy that has had to be spent elsewhere is now yours to choose where it is to be expended. Money may be short but there is the currency of time now, loads of it. And the choices are not only endless but they are yours to make. And yet... Discombobulation. Disorientation. Distraction.

Creating some sense of routine

I realized rather early in my journey in retirement that I had to have some sense of routine if I was going to "do this right." I listened ever so carefully to the stories of those who had retired ahead of me. I tried to imagine their daily lives. What did a normal day for them look like, sound like, feel like? Was there a sigh of contentment at least every other hour? Or a rush of relief when noticing the hurried lives of those still working? Or niggling guilt while reading in the middle of the day on a couch? Or walking at 2 pm through a pleasant copse? If you aren't on a grand trip but noodling around at home, what exactly are you doing? Years of working and multi-tasking have seared these accounting habits into me and, I am sure, many others. Some people find their routine in activities that take them necessarily out of the house: classes, fitness clubs, organizations requiring meetings. To be somewhere at a certain time and place — like a bit of work. I dutifully signed up for six-week art classes, three-month Tai Chi, cello lessons, and a semester of community choir, but found myself resenting slightly the need to be at a certain place at a certain time. What?! I wanted these things (presumably) so why was I silently protesting?

Puzzling it out

Alas, I can't offer any solutions because I am still working it out and, for some retirees, it will take longer to adjust to the riches of a new life (yes, it is possible to almost curse one's liberation from the work world). You think of all the hours you spent at work, perhaps taking work home and thinking and dreaming work. Suddenly it is up to you to fill these hours and do so productively, profitably, happily — a daunting task when your mindset during the great majority of your waking hours has been so long established. Even more puzzling, you have been seeking this out and dreaming about it for a considerably long time, so what is the problem? Why does retirement not feel like nirvana?

Balancing routine and the delicious lapse into flow

My strategy is to think of what makes a successful day — a lot of moments of gratitude, joy, anticipation, even the full brunt of sadness — and consider the responsibility I have in creating it. The accounting of time must be left behind and if I can't help myself and notice that I "wasted" an entire day, I am given another chance tomorrow, a whole new clean page. Success is defined differently from how I have known it for the past number of years. I may have spent two hours writing a letter which will make hardly any difference to but one individual in the world, but its work brought me a visit with a friend. Cello practice often done in a swirl of blue air with teeth clenched is brought to its knees when I listen to the sound I am making and try without too much self-immolation to create the sound I want. The euphoria of getting lost in what I am doing lifts me out of that working self which was always on alert. Mihaly Csikszentmihalyi, author of *Finding Flow: The Psychology of Engagement with Everyday Life,* suggests that discovering the activity and mindset which allows one to be absorbed in a task or pastime is key to having what he calls excellence in life. I know this: removing the lists from my life is hard because, like nearly everyone else in this world, I have intentions and goals and dreams. Figuring out the balance between necessary routines and the delicious lapse into flow is my job — at least for now.

Inertia in retirement

By Mariella Hoy

Overview

We can embrace healthy, creative inertia that feeds our dreams, rather than forcing ourselves into rigid, over-achieving routines or drifting uneasily into idleness.

I'm hearing a tune being sung by new retirees, those still adjusting to being retired. The song is about fighting inertia and the words go something like this:

I haven't played the bagpipes, like I thought I would,

I haven't gotten fit, and I really, really should,

I haven't volunteered, as good retirees do,

And my novel is blank pages — it is no good.

Coffee time is stretching, the paper must be read,

I love watching TV, especially while in bed.

Why am I so lazy; I'm playing way too much,

I had such dreams, such dreams; but now can't move ahead.

I confess, I felt inertia as I sat on the couch, thinking about writing this article. I felt that the concepts were too big: The Law of Inertia, the Self-Determination Theory, and Taoism. Too much. I brewed some coffee. I wrote a grocery list. I went outside to see the daffodils. I talked to the cat.

Fighting the Law of Inertia

Do you sometimes find yourself in a state of inertia, with one day drifting into another and not much to show for it? A vague uneasiness drifting into your consciousness?

One definition of inertia, is "the indisposition to motion, exertion, or changes." The Law of Inertia states that "unless acted upon by an external force, an object at rest remains at rest, or if in motion, it continues to move in a straight line with constant speed."

How are we to break out of this Law of Inertia? It's a law, after all. Having retired from The Job and without people telling us what to do, what gets us going? How can we boost that intrinsic motivation they tell us is so important to reaching the big dreams we have...or think we should have?

Not to Worry — we're internally programmed: The Self-Determination Theory

Well, apparently, we have three needs that carry us along our merry way: a need for autonomy, a need for competence, and a need for psychological relatedness. Autonomy: we try to control the outcomes of our experiences. Competence: we seek to be causal agents in our own lives and to act in harmony with our internal selves. And psychological relatedness: we want to be connected to others in caring relationships. We are, thus, internally programmed to take on challenges, to grow, and to strive. Ah, we can stop worrying.

Too much striving, however, can be as bad as too much inertia. Which brings me to Taoism.

The Taoist Twist

According to Frederic Henry Balfour in The Wisdom of Taoism, everything already has its own nature within it. We need to live in harmony with our nature, to imitate Mother Nature.

> *Nature never strives; therefore the Sage should guard himself from striving too. Nature is ever passive; therefore the Sage should let things take their course, contenting himself with following in their wake.*[1]

There! Our inertia has been sanctioned and blessed! Amen. I should have remained on the couch and let this article write itself.

And that leaves me confused. What about self-determination and our needs for autonomy, competence, and relatedness? The Self-Determination Theory tells us that people with high levels of intrinsic motivation have a higher level of happiness. Taoism tells us that happiness depends upon remaining passive. How can we follow the Taoist principle of not striving, yet be on the lookout for ways to boost our intrinsic motivation? Once again, we face the challenge of balancing the yin and yang of life.

---

1 Balfour, F.B. (1884). Taoist Texts: Ethical Political and Speculative. London and Shanghai. p. i. Retrieved August 19, 2022, from https://sacred-texts.com/tao/ttx/ttx01.htm

Three thoughts about dreams that seem far away

What we can take from this, perhaps, is that if we force ourselves, we run into trouble. If our big dreams aren't in line with our inner natures, then we are forcing ourselves. And if we are overdoing autonomy, competence, and relatedness, then we are forcing ourselves. Forcing spells trouble.

We're the same people after retirement as before. Our natures don't change. Add to that the lack of structure in our days, that same structure that made us so productive at work, and we're going to feel adrift at times. Excited and motivated, but adrift.

My take on it (and Taoists may suck in their breaths at this) is that our dreams aren't going to come true by themselves. So, my striving little soul has these thoughts for your consideration:

1. **The inertia we feel could mean we're in a creative stage**

   I like to think that some of the inertia we feel is the quiet gestation of creativity. The embryos of brilliance need undisturbed, rich, fertile soil. The seedlings won't sprout until they are ready. One key ingredient is social support. Our apparent idleness during this period of outward unproductiveness needs to be understood and supported.

   As Leonardo da Vinci put it, *"Men of lofty genius when they are doing the least work are most active."*

2. **Maybe we've chosen the wrong dream**

   Some of that inertia might be related to doubt about what we really want. The dreams we had while working may not scratch the itch we now have.

   I make the case for spending time being unsure of where we want to head next. Sometimes it's better to spend time in the place of not knowing, instead of making a hasty, ill-judged decision. The passionate exercise of dancing in doubt strengthens our self-awareness. Spending time in the place of not knowing lets us explore ourselves: our strengths, needs, desires, the conditions we need to thrive, and our fit in the world. This clarity about ourselves and our ideal world allows us to discover where we will thrive — the place where we can play at what we do best.

   It may take some time to figure out which dream to pursue, but once we do, our intrinsic motivation will be higher, and the process will seem effortless.

3. **The dream may seem too big**

If you're anything like me, the big projects get pushed to the back burner. The same is true for big dreams. It's easier to do the little task — send an email, clean the sink — than to tackle the scarier, but more rewarding, dreams. Getting back to playing the piano, joining the board of a non-profit organization, learning to fly an airplane... these endeavours require thought and energy.

Maybe our big dreams need to be broken down into bite-size pieces. Sharpen the pencil, get the pad of paper out. Or make one phone call. Baby steps.

Some people find it helpful to work backwards... to establish what the dream would look like in full fruition and figure out the steps backwards.

And as my wise eldest sister said, it's too hard to muscle through on willpower alone; we need to create a routine, a regular pattern of activity that gets us where we want to go.

Embracing inertia in retirement

We have highly developed skills for being productive, working hard, and having great things to show for it. Retirement might save us — it might be the time we learn to stop. To listen. To live mindfully, in full possession of all our senses. We can still be motivated to follow our dreams, but by being more in tune with the world within us and around us, the pursuits we choose to follow will be more in tune with our values and interests.

Inertia still manages to dig its powerful claws into me. I am moving in the right direction, though. – Pauline

Freedom sixty-one

By Pauline Hodge
Retired Airline Reservations Agent

Overview

Pauline's story gives us an example of how someone who loves to be active —
often physically active — builds new routines after 35 years of full-time work,
and how she copes with the unrest that comes with free time.

If time is money, I became extremely rich two years ago. On April Fool's Day, I retired. The pit pony had been released from the mines, and danced skittishly, blinking in the light. Suddenly I had about fifty extra hours in my week to do whatever I wanted to do.

Impulsively, I jumped on my bike and went for a spin around the neighbourhood. Without gloves on. It started to snow. (This is Canada, after all. And it was April Fool's Day.) By the time I got home again, my fingers were numb and clumsy and painful with cold. But I was happy.

I have worked full time for roughly thirty-five years. That adds up to a lot of packed lunches, and countless bus and subway commutes. For the last twenty-eight years (which includes three maternity leaves), I worked for one company. Over the years there, I got to know a large, diverse, talented group of people that became my work family.

The evolving schedule

Two years have flown by since the farewell party on my last day. I'm still adjusting to this drastic life change. I now wake up a bit later in the morning, and have the luxury of dawdling over the newspaper. Most mornings, I take a short walk through the park, followed by a bit of outdoor Tai Chi while the birds chirp in the trees. I continue to take the martial arts classes that I was doing before retirement, and have added a couple more. So, you will find me doing an hour of karate, kobudo (weapons) or tai chi at the dojo five days a week.

Sundays start with a 7K run, followed by breakfast and a shower. Then I attend church services, where I have temporarily taken on the responsibility of organizing the various volunteers for the 10 a.m. Mass.

This still leaves quite a bit of free time. Having no externally imposed schedule is a whole new ballgame. Our three children are in their twenties now. Two have left home; the youngest is teetering on the edge of the nest, preparing for lift-off.

I now share my days with my musician husband, who practises several hours a day on various instruments, and plays in about four different bands. He and I seem to have adjusted well to spending more time together. We often go out for lunch or catch a movie matinee. We've bought an art gallery membership, so we can visit any exhibit that appeals to us. I chauffeur him to some of his practices and performances. (His preference in instruments leans toward the bulkier, heavier ones like tuba and bassoon. "Play flute!" I suggest, but he doesn't listen.)

Stuff we've done

Last summer we added two raised beds to our backyard garden, and planted a variety of veggies, herbs, and flowers. We also participated in a week of music camp — a stimulating experience we hope to repeat this summer.

I have joined a book club, which meets once a month for lively conversation over coffee. I often meet up with former colleagues, some retired, some still working. I still attend parties at my old workplace, and catch up on gossip.

When my father became terminally ill the summer after I retired, I was able to visit frequently and assist in his care. It was a difficult, emotional time, but I was glad that I could share the caretaking and sadness with him and the family. This was not possible eleven years previously, when my mother was going through her last illness. As the main breadwinner of my family, I was unable to travel to her bedside as often as I would have liked.

It has been great having the freedom to attend a happier event... my stepson Harry's wedding in Vietnam thirteen months ago. As of January 12th, we have a new little grandbaby in Ho Chi Minh City to enjoy, although, so far, we've only seen her via Skype.

However...

We are adjusting to a reduced income now that I have retired. The health and dental benefits are also reduced, which seems like the wrong way around now that we are getting older. It's a great blessing to have a mortgage-free home. The house needs many repairs, though, and our vehicle is now fifteen years old.

At almost sixty-nine, my husband's health is not wonderful. He pants after climbing one set of stairs, and his arthritic knees give him chronic pain. His walking speed has slowed dramatically in the last few years.

My plans to travel, paint, join an acting group of some kind and write have not yet materialized. Inertia is powerful; it's easier to do all the puzzles in the newspaper and watch a TV show than get down to some creative endeavour. The deadline for a short story contest came and went, and all I had to show for it was an opening paragraph. Signing up for a class would likely help me to get started.

As a retiree, I sometimes feel like an outsider peering through an invisible window at the world of the employed. Already I have forgotten procedures and transactions that I used to use daily. Unlike those in the working world, I now have the luxury of choice; on the coldest, iciest days of winter, I can choose to shovel snow, scrape the car windshield, negotiate slippery roads during rush hour, trudge on foot through snowbanks... or I can simply stay at home. The stresses associated with a full-time job have disappeared; I no longer have to remind myself to relax my shoulders and breathe deeply.

But too much free time makes me restless. I've contemplated finding part-time work, to add a bit more structure and social contact to my days, and provide a little extra pocket cash.

Meanwhile...

Meanwhile, I enjoy the freedom to make last-minute plans and act impulsively. I flew to Ottawa last winter to see our daughter perform in a play, and the next day fulfilled a long-held ambition to skate on the Rideau Canal. Such fun! So cold! In summertime, in the middle of the week, I've been able to stroll by the riverside in Guelph with two of my sisters, all three of us licking ice cream cones.

Recently, things came full circle. Before breakfast, I got the bike out for the first ride of the year... an hour-long cycle through a large nearby park. Ice and snow still clung to some parts of the trail (this is Canada, after all). One trail-walker eyed me dubiously and murmured with a smile, "Crazy!" Not so crazy, really — I was wearing warm gloves this time.

Upon retiring, I felt disoriented for a very long time as I became accustomed to realizing that time really does belong to me, for possibly the first time in my life. – Rose

Responses to the question "What do you do all day?"

I heard from retired people that too often they are accosted by working stiffs with this: "Retired, eh? So, what do you do all day?" Often, it is obvious that the person asking the question considers them to be a lesser mortal now that they no longer hold a place in the working world. Bored, the working person asks the question anyway: What do you do all day?

In order for us to have responses ready in advance, I asked my newsletter subscribers to come up with witty or sarcastic suggestions. Here are a few for you to consider.

Question:

Retired, eh? So, what do you do all day?

Answers:

- Do you mean when I'm not having sex?
- I'm learning to be, not to do.
- Am I retired? Cripes, I thought I was dead and in heaven.
- All day? How quaint. I haven't done anything all day in... what was the question again?
- I turn off the alarm and roll over.
- What I can say with complete conviction is that when the day is done, I've done everything that had to be done.
- I watch Netflix and eat bon bons.
- I do everything you wish you could do.
- What would you do if you had a little free time? I have endless time.
- It sounds as though you think it's a problem to be paid to decide how you're going to spend your time. I hope you're going to have that problem. I worry about you and your generation.
- I've stopped measuring my worth by what I do.
- Oh, you mean I have nothing to offer you?
- For one thing, I'm no longer controlled by the puritan work ethic.
- Ya, I used to think that work was the only source of value too, that my job defined me. That is so not the case!
- I tune into the evening rush hour traffic report and chuckle, being careful not to spill my gin and tonic on the crossword.
- Imagine your best vacation. Now, imagine it not ending.
- Have you got enough in your RRSP to be even asking that question?

? Self-Coaching Questions

It takes time for an individual to create a new world of possibilities, to imagine and bring into being that which has never before existed, the wonder of a full and realized life. – Wade Davis

Rebuilding Routines

What do you (or did you) like about your work routines that you'd like to recreate in retirement? What didn't you like about your work routines that you'd like to leave behind?

If you were to list all your daily and weekly activities, which ones would be favourites for you? How can you schedule time for those?

When in the past have you been so focused on an activity that you lost track of time? How can you build that activity into your new routines?

What can you build into your new routines that focus on...

(a) your mind?

(b) your body?

(c) your soul?

If you have a partner at home, how might you each spend 4 hours a day doing something apart from the other?

Following Frank into retirement:
3 months to go

Money, money, money — being responsible

I have already mentioned my obsession with cash flow spreadsheets and my money worries. Instead of fixating on that, I thought I would share some bits of information that have eased my mind as a result of discussing our financial situation with family, friends, and our investment advisor.

You say tomato, I say...

I quickly learned that everyone has a different opinion about what they need in retirement. We've decided to keep our life simple, primarily because our lifestyle always has been simple. We've never wanted to own a cottage or a winter retreat in the south, don't take long or multiple exotic vacations, or even need two cars because of divergent interests. We do want a comfortable, attractive house. Some modest travel is desirable and comes with the bonus of getting to research and plan our trip beforehand. We also like to eat well (and feed people), so we've made sure there is plenty of room in the budget to buy those nice cheeses, lots of chocolate, wine and scotch, and all those exotic ingredients we need to create our favourite dishes. I guess you could call us homebodies. I'm sure our lifestyle would cause others to pale at the thought, but my point is that you have to figure out what you need to be true to yourself over the next few decades. Buying into someone else's dreams of retirement could cause you to either over- or underestimate the amount you need in the bank before retiring.

May you live to be 120

I expect that I will live to be somewhere between 85 and 90 years old. Suzanne, on the other hand, is aiming to fulfill the Yiddish birthday wish of "may you live bis ein hunnert und zwanzig" (until 120). My spreadsheet split the difference and mapped out all our financial needs until I was 100, at which time our only asset would be the house in which we now live.

When we met with our investment advisor, his canned software only calculated cash flows up to 90 years of age. Although his model showed that we would have plenty of money left in our estate at age 90, it did not include about $100,000 that I anticipated we would need to fix up our house in 2036 or the cost of living for the next 10 years. His answer set me back on my heels: "They don't include capital costs past 80 or living expenses past 90 because there is no possible way for anyone to predict the future with any accuracy."

Of course, it's important that you have funds to cover your living expenses, but will we still be physically able to live in our house? Will we still want to live in our house? Will the economy be up or down? Will I eat a dodgy leftover from the fridge and shuffle off my mortal coil at age 72? Much to my chagrin, we will just have to adapt as best as we can to whatever life throws at us.

Inheritance guilt

Besides being comfortable with our lifestyle, my only other major financial concern is not being able to leave a whack of cash to our children when we're gone. Our parents worked hard to provide for us, and our early retirement is partly owing to our inheritances from them. My conscience has had a field day lecturing me about my duty to pass along to my children at least as much as our parents did to us (and of equivalent value, not inflated dollars). Without money they will be nothing! I was so perturbed by my guilt that I went to the root of the problem and asked my kids what they thought of our early retirement and the squandering of their inheritance. While I did not expect them to say that we should work until we drop, I was relieved to have them honestly answer that, while getting some money later would be nice, they are not counting on it. We should do whatever makes us happiest. They are adults. They are getting their own lives going. We are responsible only to continue to give them unconditional love, support, and friendship as we all live our lives.

So, talk about your retirement plans with those people who are most important to you and whose opinion you value. It will help shape your vision of retirement which in turn will make it clearer what funds you need to retire. Since life has a way of mucking with the best laid plans, do your best, and then, in the words of Bobby McFerrin, "Don't worry, be happy."

4 Adapting to Illness and Limitations

The COVID-19 influenza pandemic gave us a swift and relentless lesson in illness and limitations. Three generations of my sister-in-law's family were infected with the virus, some of them twice. She, her husband, and oldest son were hospitalized. So sick they were! Fortunately, their conditions did not necessitate intubation and they were soon released and, although they were exhausted and ill for weeks, they didn't face the limitations that COVID long-haulers have faced.

The pandemic restrictions, mask wearing, social distancing, and stay-at-home orders taught us a new meaning of limitations. Forced to sacrifice our personal freedoms for the good of our communities, many endured isolation, boredom, anxiety, and depression.

All that came on top of the regular illnesses and limitations we face in retirement, as a result of aging and chronic conditions.

I'm not very good at dealing with the limitations that come with aging. I'm not reconciled to aging gracefully.

As my daughter Sylvie said, "Limitations stink!" However, she went on to say, in her young wisdom, "But opportunities abound." When she had to leave behind playing in a band, playing rugby, and rowing on her varsity rowing team, she said, "Inevitably, I found another thing I loved to devote my energy to."

It is on that positive note that I gathered the articles for this chapter. We'll look at how a professor fought off stress, exhaustion, and major depression and narrowly escaped involuntary early retirement. Her tale ends with a cautionary note. Then, you can read about the struggle to balance r-aging and aging gracefully. After that, we have an article by a hospice chaplain who tells of how one fiercely productivity-oriented resident turned her life limitations into new challenges. And, finally, you can dip into my self-therapy on the day I was diagnosed with osteoporosis.

Articles in this chapter:

- *Staving off involuntary retirement: The emotional side*
- *Aging: I haven't been reading the script*
- *Redefining competence: Ponderings from a hospice chaplain*
- *Dealing with the wild cards*
- *Self-coaching questions*

Staving off involuntary early retirement: The emotional side

By Helen
Retired University Professor of English and Women's Studies

Overview

Stress, exhaustion, and major depression forced a 3-year leave of absence for Helen, and almost forced her into early retirement. Hers is a cautionary tale.

At the height of my academic career, I found myself on the outside looking in. After meetings with my GP, my Chair, my Dean, and the doctor at Occupational Health, I was suddenly on medical leave. I had no idea if it would be a week, a month, or forever. Stress, exhaustion, major depression. That wasn't how I wanted my career to end. Lots of unfinished business. Lots of shame, however inappropriate. With my colleagues overburdened in my absence, I felt I was letting down the team.

Ultimately, I was able to choose when I retired. I want to explore the changes in my emotional life and in my relationship to work that allowed me to defer retirement until I was ready for it.

My advantages

I was lucky. I had an understanding and respectful doctor. I had a good income and savings. I had a loving partner and supportive friends and family. I had a hitherto good brain and a good education. I had race and class privilege. I had a union. I had disability insurance.

Mind you, my good income was part of the devil's bargain made by many professionals: lots of money and no life — or at least little time in which to enjoy it. My disability insurance created problems that only added to my stresses; the ongoing need to prove my disability forced a focus on illness and incapacity at a time when my recovery depended on the opposite. Still, I was very lucky.

Coddled

A workaholic, I spent the first week of my leave disentangling myself, labouring through one last promised task. Then I could collapse. For the first week of actual recovery, I deliberately treated myself as a convalescent from surgery, lying on the couch, listening to music, and relying on my partner to feed me soft foods (coddled eggs, canned green beans — I know, I know!). Thereafter, along with the music,

I listened to relaxation tapes and did daily breathing exercises and a bit of meditation. Because of the waiting list for a grief support group, I did my own grief work for half an hour or more daily, first around my mother's death, then around the losses and pain associated with my daughter's fetal-alcohol condition.

At the beginning, supposedly simple, restful activities like Scrabble and solitaire sometimes proved too difficult or disheartening, threatening to intensify my depression. Although I continued my routine half-hour run every weekday morning, sometimes I had to draw on reserves of willpower not to just lie down in the snow and stay there.

Learning to expect less

I attended monthly meetings of a Fetal Alcohol parent support group, a better source of helpful information and practical strategies than all the professionals. There I learned the characteristics of my daughter's brain damage and how to accommodate them. I learned to speak less and recognize silence as companionable, to simplify her environment, to anticipate stresses, to expect less, and to make the many adjustments away from conventional parenting necessary with FASD. For my own mental health, I also learned to resist projecting into the future, to try to give up controlling what I could not, to pair stress with extra sleep, and eventually to put my painful experience to broader positive use in the community as an FASD advocate and educator.

A new balance

I worked my way through the many helpful assignments on creativity in Julia Cameron's *The Artist's Way,* a project which requires a year off work to be manageable. Three daily pages of morning notes proved therapeutic. And I took art lessons. My dream had always been to be a novelist, and I'd written a few short stories. But my own knowledge of literature inhibited me. Although I couldn't doodle a twig successfully, a drawing class proved to me that, if I used my eye rather than my memory, I could sketch a convincing hand or bottle or human figure, even. Painting became my new creative outlet.

Exposure to a rigid form of Catholicism had alienated me from institutional religions. In the wilderness after my mother's death, I found an earth-based spirituality, a version of paganism (though that term perturbs many), that required not belief but a sense of my place in the cycles of transformation, of the moon, of the seasons, of "birth, initiation, love, repose, and death." I was lucky enough as well to find a group within which to practise the rituals of this spirituality. So I began balancing my intellectual life with attention to my emotional, artistic, and spiritual sides.

Undressing core beliefs

Reluctantly, but for many years, I took medication to restore my serotonin and norepinephrine levels. When the next available cognitive-therapy group turned out not to be sufficiently anonymous, I used a library cognitive-therapy workbook to help train myself out of damaging core beliefs. Cognitive-therapy exercises are extensive: what core beliefs underlie this feeling? What is the evidence for this belief? What is the evidence against it? What would be a more accurate formulation? How strongly do you feel the emotion now? Eventually just the threat of having to slog through the exercises would sometimes be enough to head off negative ruminations. After a series of psychiatrists prescribed by my insurance company, I continued with a counsellor covered by my Employee Assistance Plan. With her I developed a list of crisis strategies, including the employee crisis line, for the inside of my closet door. Having the list, without using it, proved sufficient. From there we went on to emotional exploration.

Hardening off & post-traumatic growth

Towards the end of my three years of leave, the insurance plan referred me to a therapist specifically for "work-hardening," a horrifying term but fortunately with a person I could trust. We worked on approaches to reduce work anxieties, desensitize me to the campus (which I'd been avoiding), compensate for memory problems, resist obsessiveness, and modify my improvisational teaching style.

Over the years of my leave, I learned that there is such a thing as post-traumatic growth. I learned, by necessity, to balance my life, to breathe, to be mindfully in the present, to distract my amygdala (and its fight-flight-freeze reaction) with mental puzzles, to find creative and spiritual outlets, and to build a network of support. Every so often, especially after long winters, I still need to take preventative action to ward off depression.

Anticipate your cracking point

For one of my siblings and several of my friends, disability has meant the unwelcome, abrupt, early end to their work lives. So I understand that only some forms of disability can be anticipated and forestalled. In my case, I wonder if I could have protected myself better. My discoveries are nothing surprising, all familiar remedies available to me before my crisis. The lessons here are more, I suppose, about drawing on these insights before the shattering. If you want to retire only at the end of your working life, know your cracking point. And then make the changes (if those changes are within your control — and they aren't always), while that point is still in the far distance. Resist the false assurances of your inner superwoman. Keeping work in perspective, as part of a richer, gentler life, allowed me to enjoy working longer.

> **❝**
>
> *I've learned the value of creating a peaceful harbour for myself in the world. There is nothing quite like coming through a life storm safely, to a place of acceptance and contentment.*
>
> *– Nancy*
>
> **❞**

Aging: I haven't been reading the script

By Mariella Hoy

Overview

In adapting to the limitations that come with aging, in this article I question the 'aging gracefully' approach and crankily encourage a little 'raging against the dying of the light.'

Having been rather tired recently, for no apparent reason, I said to my twin brother, "Do you think that our age is one of the reasons we feel tired more often?" He said, "Of course!" I said, "I'm not really ready to agree that age is a factor in my tiredness." He responded, "You haven't been asked to agree. It's in the script."

I guess I haven't been reading the script.

My last foray onto the little theatre stage was as the fox in Green Eggs and Ham. A friend who watched the play said, "You can really move. I thought you were one of the teenagers." Onstage, I had forgotten that I was then almost 60. The reality is, though, that the play, being only 14 minutes long, was short enough to sustain the illusion of youth.

Sneaky offstage prompts

Sneaky little cues are being whispered by life's prompter offstage... you're getting older, you can't expect to jump around like a teenager, you can't remember your lines. I now have a tricky knee and, although I can still (almost) carry a canoe, it's more bravado than real strength. I'm getting the dates wrong for my nieces' and nephews' birthdays and it's not that I forget them, it's that I recorded them in the calendar incorrectly. I can't always trust my brain!

When I was 59 years old, I rashly committed to a push-up contest with my daughter on my 60th birthday. Four months later, I could do only half the number of push-ups that I could when I started preparing. As I trained, physiotherapist at my side, I was exacerbating chronic cartilage inflammation along my sternum, and creating a painful knot of muscles in my trapezius. The physiotherapist said I needed to lower my goals. I was then only doing five push-ups. What the hell!

Aging Gracefully

When I discussed my crankiness about aging with my brother-in-law, he said that there is merit in aging gracefully. The concept holds great appeal and brings to mind the image of a wise elder who has "...the serenity to accept the things she cannot change, the courage to change the things she can, and the wisdom to know the difference." This wise elder would be someone who knows pain and suffering, but has moved beyond them, someone who keeps active and optimistic in spite of roadblocks, and someone who gracefully lets go the things of youth.

Did Dick Van Dyke age gracefully?

At 89 years of age, actor-singer-dancer Dick Van Dyke said he simply ignored the less enjoyable parts of aging. His advice was to keep moving.

His motivation for fitness changed as he aged. In his thirties he wanted to look good, in his fifties he wanted to stay fit, in his seventies he wanted to stay ambulatory, and in his eighties he wanted to avoid assisted living. He figured that exercising in his nineties would be an act of defiance.

Ignore the bad, keep moving, sing and dance... is that how to age gracefully?

But what happened to "Rage, rage against the dying of the light"?

Didn't the Welsh poet Dylan Thomas say, "Do not go gentle into that good night"? Are we not to "Rage, rage against the dying of the light"? Rage is certainly not my natural inclination, but I suspect it underlies the grouchiness I feel each time I smack up against an age roadblock, whether it be physical or mental.

I don't feel like being graceful. I don't want to be adult-like — accepting and adjusting. Like a child who kicks and screams when told not to climb onto the table, I'd prefer to rant at new restrictions. (I guess that's what I'm doing now. Sorry.) But why can't I rage, rage against the dying of the light? Instead of aging gracefully, I want to be r-aging!

Though what is there to rage about — really? I don't fear death, at least I don't think I do. I only fret at new restrictions. And restrictions are nothing new. We've faced new restrictions daily, from when we took our first baby steps. How is aging, and adjusting to new restrictions, any different as a 60- or 70-year-old?

Are we stuck with the script?

I guess what I fear in following the script and listening to the prompter offstage is that I'll not maintain the determination to keep taking up challenges, to keep trying new things, and to keep doing all I used to do. By letting go gracefully, would I be prone to being less than I can be? (Now, there's a measurement word: less. Who is measuring and what is being measured?)

Perhaps I need to reframe what getting old means. Doesn't it mean taking on new roles? Some never could carry a canoe (and who would want to anyway?) Does not carrying a canoe anymore matter? Does not running anymore change the essentials?

Just do your own thing. Go to racing school. Stay weird.

From what I see, aging raises many questions, it is different for everyone, and no one has definitive answers.

To celebrate 11 years on air, CBC Radio's *WireTap* show created a farewell video called *How to Age Gracefully*. This short video offers words of wisdom from people of all ages to their younger counterparts.

I liked the 91-year-old's advice to do your own thing, no matter what others advise. She figured nobody knows what they are doing anyway. A 53-year-old woman decided to go to car racing school - using her husband's Corvette. A 7-year-old advised that we stay weird, no matter what anyone says.

Advice to myself

1. **List all the things I liked and am missing about the old way,**

   e.g., Running gave me good health, strength, confidence, and feel-good endorphins.

   e.g., I liked having confidence in my memory.

2. **For each thing I'm missing, find three ways to replace it,**

   e.g., Maintain my good health by walking fast, cross-country skiing, and doing yoga.

   e.g., Use computer reminders and lists, use memory cues to remember names of people I've just met, have a good quip ready for when I mess up.

3. **Be completely honest and list all the things I like about the new way,**

    e.g., Walking is easy, it lets me appreciate more fully what's around me, and it doesn't require a shower and clothing change when done.

    e.g., It's a relief to have backup for my faulty memory and it takes a load off my mind.

It's time to stop whingeing, get off my lard arse, and start enjoying my new roles. And maybe I can edit the script to suit my character as I go along.

Time speeds up later in life. Two days ago, I filled my weekly pill dispenser and today it needs filling again. – Helen

Redefining competence: Ponderings from a hospice chaplain

By *Kathy Underwood*
Retired United Church Minister and Hospice Spiritual Care Provider

---

Overview

Kathy tells us of how one woman reframed her sense of self and what held meaning for her, when facing the ultimate limitation — death.

Note: To protect confidentiality, this story is a composite of several individuals' stories.

There are few things more satisfying to me as spending time with people who are facing their own vulnerability and who allow me to accompany them for a while. As a spiritual care provider, it is my privilege to hear the stories people share and to respond with questions that help them to consider the deeper meanings underlying their concerns, their fears, and their hopes. In turn, I have discovered my own deep-seated vulnerabilities, fears, and hopes. This has given me the opportunity to address them proactively before I face the threat of serious illness or my own mortality — a tremendous gift to me and to those around me. These are some of the insights I have gleaned:

What does it mean to be productive?

Louise is a 64-year-old woman who has been active all her life. She retired as a successful business owner one year ago and was looking forward to pursuing her lifelong passions of golfing, photography, and downhill skiing. Shortly after her retirement she was diagnosed with a form of leukemia that has robbed her of her energy and her previously-boundless passion for life. We talked at length one day about how we define ourselves. Louise was clear her identity had always been focused on her capacity to be productive and successful. Even her stress management activities had been practiced at an elite level where others could see her competence as a golfer, a downhill skier, and photographer. Now she saw no competence and no capacity when she considered her life. Although she maintained a strong fighting attitude toward her disease, she spoke judgmentally and hopelessly about her current self.

Our talks together focused on achieving a new understanding of competence, capacity, and productivity. Can I be flexible and compassionate enough with myself to see my new 'work' as being as healthy as I can be, regardless of my limitations? Can I see this flexibility and adjustment to limitations as being a sign of my competence? Can I prioritize becoming competent in knowing how and when to ask for help?

My time spent with Louise and many others facing similar physical limitations is helping me to revisit my own understanding of who I am and what makes my life worthwhile. I am becoming much more compassionate with myself and others regarding productivity and success. This compassion is helping me to face my own limitations with an attitude that doesn't take away from my goal-focused, outcome-oriented approach, but that allows space for seeing goals and outcomes in a much broader context. And in so doing, creates a much larger space for hope.

I've got the gift of time. Unfortunately, there is an expiry date to this gift, so I want to spend it wisely. – Frank

Dealing with the wild cards

By Mariella Hoy

Overview

It seems I'm cranky again. This time, a diagnosis of osteoporosis is the cause. In this article, I review my thinking on the day I received the news, from catastrophizing to determination, if not hopefulness.

It was hard to know just what to think when my doctor's office called and asked me to come in to discuss my test results. When I saw the doctor, she said, "We've got to talk about your bone density. You've got significant osteoporosis." Wow, I thought! Now that's a wild card! Out of the blue. Unexpected.

My lab report indicated that within the next 10 years there is an intermediate risk that I will break a bone. I know what that will feel like, having broken many bones in my childhood: both arms, both legs, and two chipped vertebrae. They hurt. And then they heal. The only difference is that, next time I break a bone, it won't heal as easily because the bones have become fragile. The break may become infected. I may develop a blood clot while bedridden, leading to a stroke. I might develop a dowager's hump. Become wheelchair bound. Okay, I'm catastrophizing. I'm just a little bummed out, I guess.

Contemplating the timeline

It takes time to process this kind of information. At home on my couch, I contemplate. My cats contemplate me. The leaves continue to fall from the trees. The sun continues to shine. But I feel a shift in my perception of my world. I see a shortened timeline. It's not that the timeline has changed; it's only that I now see the timeline more clearly.

I recognize how self-indulgent my thoughts are. Lots of people have osteoporosis. After looking into it, I discovered an estimated 10% of Canadians 40 years of age or older reported having been diagnosed with osteoporosis. One in three women will suffer a fracture from osteoporosis in their lifetime. One in five men. With most of these people, their osteoporosis will go undiagnosed and untreated. Twenty-eight per cent of women and 37% of men who suffer a hip fracture will die within the following year. I imagine these are older people though, not spry young things like me!

I know the news could have been much worse. I know my loss is not a big deal when compared to the life and death struggle my father fought with cancer. He had to adjust to the final limitation — the certainty that life would soon end. My loss is nothing compared to the limitations faced by a friend who lost his life partner. Or compared to the many people who are suddenly laid off from work in their mid-50s. Not to mention my colleague with multiple sclerosis or my neighbour with quadriplegia. I could be one of the many people diagnosed with dementia, bipolar disorder, or any number of horrible diseases. Worst of all, I could be one of those parents whose child has been diagnosed with a nasty terminal illness.

That doesn't stop me from being ticked off! I have still to find my own way through the disappointment and loss. I have still to run the circuit of grief: denial, anger, bargaining, depression, and acceptance. Currently, my favourites are denial and anger.

Choosing how long to sit in the puddle

There's nothing wrong with sitting in a puddle of denial, anger, or resistance. I need a chance to work through my thoughts and emotions. I've heard that anger, for instance, masks helplessness, and we need to burn out the anger before we can deal with our helplessness. We can, at the same time, find ways to soothe our souls, through beauty and other people's goodness. The trick is not to stagnate, not to stay too long in the puddle.

An ever-changing hand of cards

Will this diagnosis change how I live today? Maybe a little. I'll do what my doctor says — I'll take 2000 UIs of vitamin D, I'll increase my intake of calcium to 1500 mg per day, and I'll walk more. The good news... I love milk, cheese, eggs, English muffins, kale, and yogurt... no boring dairy-free or gluten-free diet for me! And maybe this wake-up call will only intensify my enjoyment of life — the appreciation of dark chocolate squares melting in my mouth, the warmth of a duvet fresh from the dryer, the view of ice-encased crabapples through my window. Instead of focusing on the dark possibilities, receiving a wild card can lead me to live each moment with more clarity and vitality.

All that has happened is that, once again, I am facing a new limitation — or a new opportunity, as my better-adjusted friend would say. We can expect our health to diminish. And, when it does, we create opportunities to reconstruct what we've lost, but in new ways. We focus on others instead of ourselves. We remain hopeful. Eventually, I find, we revert to our normal emotional equilibrium. We become ourselves again. It's like a game of cards. We keep getting dealt new cards, each card changing our hand, changing our game plan. I don't want to be one of those card players who always complains about their cards, as if the card dealer is out to get them. As if their luck is any worse than anyone else's. Get on with it. Enjoy the game, for heaven's sake!

My partner has a lovely way of seeing aging and the procession of body breakdowns presented to us. He laughs. He sees the business of getting old as amusing. And he says that if we let it get to us, it can crush us. He also reminds me to be hopeful. The medical advancements are startling.

The sun is now lighting up the massive, old sugar maple outside my window. The cats are sleeping. My chest no longer feels tight. My normal good humour is reasserting itself. Thank you for being part of my therapy.

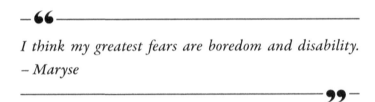

I think my greatest fears are boredom and disability.
– Maryse

Self-Coaching Questions

To be without some of the things you want is an indispensable part of happiness. – Bertrand Russell

Adapting to Illness and Limitations

Questions about recreating what you lost:

- What have you had to give up recently that you used to enjoy and are now really missing?
- What did you love about that activity (or person, pet, thing)?
- In what three ways can you recreate each of those things that you loved?
- What do you enjoy about the new way?

Questions about your body:

- What is your ideal physical activity level, given your current condition?
- If you aren't at that level now, what stands in your way?
- What supports would you need to get you moving towards that ideal?

Questions from Hospice Chaplain Kathy Underwood:

- Can you be flexible and compassionate enough with yourself to see your new 'work' as being as healthy as you can be, regardless of your limitations?
- Can you see this flexibility and adjustment to limitations as being a sign of your competence?
- Can you prioritize becoming competent in knowing how and when to ask for help?

Following Frank into Retirement:
2 months to go

So much time and so little to do

I'm a middle-of-the-road kind of guy. I enjoy both quiet and strenuous activities and have a wide range of interests, but have yet to discover one that I can pursue with passion (except, of course, Suzanne). While I'm not hyperactive or driven, I do eventually get restless if I'm not up to my elbows in something. I like doing stuff. So, in three months' time, all those activities that have kept me occupied in the evenings and on weekends will become my full-time occupation. Will it be enough?

Don't do today what you can do tomorrow

Ever since Suzanne and I decided that we would retire at roughly the same time, any large job around our house or property that needs to be done, but is not urgent, has been postponed until after we retire. Why squeeze something into our busy schedules now when we can procrastinate later? Our boxes of uninstalled kitchen backsplash tiles and grout are gathering dust. Our bush trails are overgrown. My workshop is a disaster. The gardens have been neglected and the Japanese knotweed / False spirea / Virginia creeper / brambles are not-so-slowly taking over. These are all jobs that in the past would have been done in an exhausting frenzy because of the limited time available. We are really looking forward to picking away at them over a long stretch of time. No need to flog ourselves completing a job in two days if we can devote maybe an hour or two a day over a couple of weeks to get it done. We're hoping that even the more onerous work, like weeding gardens and mowing the lawn, will become more enjoyable at a leisurely pace. Personally, I can't wait to see the impact of a long-term campaign against some of the more aggressive plants around our house. Mother Nature never rests? Well, we can be pretty persistent too!

The big leap

I talk a pretty good game, but I'm still quite concerned about the sudden shift from full work hours to full leisure hours. Besides a salary and spending power (money, arrgh!), work provides me with a focus for a major part of the day and social interaction with my colleagues. Will my ideas for life in retirement be enough to keep me happy or at least sane?

As I mentioned in earlier articles, Suzanne and I enjoy spending as much time together as possible, but we both have our work experiences to provide additional personal connections. Will we be able to find enough camaraderie from volunteer work and participating in various activities?

It would be good to start testing the waters by volunteering before retirement, but we just don't have the time or energy. In theory, there should be no problem with retirement, and in the worst case, I suppose I could always go back to working (arrgh again!). To be on the safe side, though, I am building up an inventory of things I would like to do, but for which I just haven't had the time.

Raindrops on roses and whiskers on kittens

So, these are a few of my favourite things. I love to cook (and eat) and I'm keen to build a smoker, figure out how to bake Jewish style rye bread, make my own salami, and experiment with vegetarian jerky and sausages. I love trees and I expect to spend days upon days pruning branches, building trails, and hugging trees on our 85 acres. While I may not be passionate about music, I really enjoy farting around on different instruments and I've got a baritone, a clarinet, a French horn, a trumpet, a flute, a trombone, several recorders and harmonicas, a guitar, a piano, and a harmonium (all in various states of disrepair) that should keep me tooting. I'm also keen to learn more about gas engines and car maintenance as I like to fix things, and our lawn mowers, weed whacker, chain saws, snowblower, and car will provide me with ample opportunity to do so. Reading is a great escape for me and I'm always thrilled to find a new book that turns day into night and night into day. Besides fiction, I'll be reading up on the history, culture, and customs of the various countries we intend to visit. It makes travel so much more interesting for me. I would also like to try volunteering to read to the elderly and sick.

Speaking of volunteering, you won't see me on any boards or going to meetings. I want hands-on work. Perhaps I can help out at the local food bank or Habitat Restore, or bake treats for people visiting loved ones at the nearest hospice. Of course, my list wouldn't be complete without mentioning my three favourite kids and their significant others. I'm really looking forward to having the time to spend with them. Camping, playing, plotting, renovating, babysitting (no rush!), partying — I'm up for anything they want to do with us.

5 Confronting Death

We can't escape the fact that retirement usually happens when we are older, "of a certain age." The good news is that we're not dying as soon as we retire. The shock of sudden retirement rarely kills. Most people will have a good 5 to 40 years of retirement. We're living longer and more comfortably. Our health care, education, and support systems have improved immensely over the years. We don't need to worry about those stories we hear in which people drop dead shortly after retirement.

Death happens, though, and we see its black cloak sweep by us more as we age. Two more of my friends have been diagnosed with cancer. No longer having any grandparents, aunts, or uncles still living in my family, I am now exposed on the front lines, closest to the enemy. A small virus has killed millions of people around the world. Death whispers nearby, urging us to make life count while time remains.

Let us look at this matter with eyes open and shoulders relaxed. Take a breath and we'll begin.

First, we have the story of a woman whose husband died shortly after retirement, forcing her to develop Plan B. Then, if you're interested, you can read my thoughts about grief and how I try to separate the anguish of the event from my feelings for the person. And how I attempt to translate the loss into something found. Finally, you can learn from someone who spent a good deal of thought on the subject of death and came up with a few perspectives with which to hijack our fear of death.

Articles in this chapter:
- *One widow's retirement story*
- *The graveyard in my mind*
- *Navigating the end of the bend*
- *Self-coaching questions*

One widow's retirement story

By Judy Callahan
Retired Director, Child Care Services
University of Guelph

Overview

Judy's husband Gerald died suddenly, shortly after they retired. That meant Plan B, a plan that required living without him. She tells her tale in two parts, first, 9 months after Gerald's death, and then, two years later.

Part 1: Written 9 months after Gerald's death

Four years ago, as my husband and I were beginning to consider when we might retire, I attended a retirement workshop run by Mariella. I wanted to think about how we might handle this transition in our lives with "purpose and passion". Her seminar was very informative and stimulated much discussion between my husband and me. Mariella shared that a large percentage of individuals retired, not when they had planned, but earlier, due to poor health. I was surprised to hear this, but, in fact, this is what happened to Gerald and me.

Due to his health challenges, we both retired earlier than planned. We had not reached all our financial goals for retirement; however, we were in a relatively comfortable position so we took the plunge! Fortunately, Gerald's health improved and we set about carrying out our retirement plan. We travelled, bought a fishing boat, and spent as much time as possible with our families, 13 grandchildren, and friends. Life was good, proceeding nicely according to Retirement Plan A.

Devastation

Four years later, a week before Christmas, our family received devastating news. Gerald was diagnosed with stage 4, metastatic, pancreatic cancer. He was 67 years old. He died 35 days later.

The Dreaded Plan B

Now, 9 months later, I am a 63-year-old widow trying to develop Retirement Plan B... the plan in which I continue on without him.

None of us wants a Retirement Plan B. Most of us don't want to talk about what we would do if our spouse died. Unfortunately, it is a reality that many of you will face in the future. Many of the widows/widowers I know have been left in terrible financial and emotional circumstances because there was no Plan B.

Gerald and I had done a fair bit of financial planning, but had not discussed the situation in which I now find myself. However, among all the widows I now know, I have been left in a much better position in most areas than the majority of them. I thank Gerald every day for the planning we carried out in advance.

Lessons learned the hard way

My friends ask me what advice I might give them, based on what I now know. This is what I say:

- Develop Retirement Plan A based on all the recommendations made by professionals and ensure that all your financial affairs are in order and up to date. Plan A assumes you are both alive.
- Develop a Plan B in the event that you are widowed. It is imperative that this includes a financial plan for the surviving spouse, as, in many cases, income is likely to be significantly reduced.
  - Discuss whether the remaining spouse can afford to maintain the current housing arrangement or whether there will be an immediate need to move. Many widows/widowers are forced to address this matter within months of their spouse's death when they are extremely emotionally vulnerable and perhaps least able to make sound judgments about their future.
  - Ensure that income will be immediately available to the surviving spouse so that the monthly bills and funeral expenses can be paid.
  - Ensure that, wherever possible, all bank accounts, investments, pensions, and household expenses, etc., are in both names.
  - Ensure that you have discussed what funeral plans you would both like; some couples preplan and prepay for their funerals so that the surviving spouse does not have to make all these decisions.
  - Ensure that wills, powers of attorney, and personal care directives are up to date.
  - Ensure that your executor(s) are aware of their responsibilities; if you have children, ensure that they are aware of your wishes and who will be making decisions.
  - Ensure that ALL passwords for various accounts are written down where both spouses can find them. (I cannot stress how important it is to keep this list up to date EVERY time a password is changed.
  - Prepare a list that includes all the contact information for those who must be notified that your spouse has died, for example, government agencies, pension and insurance companies, etc. Most funeral homes can provide you with a list of who should be notified.

- Discuss with your spouse what they would like you to do with their personal belongings that are especially meaningful to them, for example, where does he/she want the coin collection to go? The sports memorabilia? The fishing equipment? The sewing machine? Disposing of a spouse's belongings is an extremely painful task. Having some idea of where your spouse wants these items to go is very helpful in making this task a bit easier.
  - Many of the items in Plan B are also part of Plan A.
- Prepare a binder that includes all of the above information so the surviving spouse can easily access all pertinent information. There are books in the library that are very helpful in outlining all the items that should be included in the binder.
- Now, set aside points 1 and 2, other than conducting a yearly review of Plans A and B to update and ensure their continued viability. If your financial situation is complicated, it may be prudent to review the plan more frequently.
- Make a list of all the things you enjoy and cherish about your spouse. Be thankful for them every day... take nothing for granted! Make plans to spend quality time with one another.
- If possible, begin carrying out your retirement goals even before you retire... don't wait! There will never be a "perfect time," so start now!

Part 2: Written 3 years after Gerald's death

Plan B takes shape

Within six months of Gerald's death, almost all of the financial matters that required my attention were completed. There came a clear point when I could no longer occupy my days with paperwork related to his death. "What now?" was the question I asked myself many times a day. How would I continue to create a Plan B?

An astounding choice

I remember talking to a widower who was 14 months out from his wife's death. They had known for three years that she was dying. I remember feeling jealous that they had had three years in which to live and say goodbye. He told me many stories about their love for one another and how they had spent their last years together. And then he said something that struck me as very odd at the time. Nine months after her death, he made a decision that he wasn't going to be sad anymore. I was astounded by this statement! How does one choose not to be sad when the pain is so unbearable? My first reaction was to dismiss his comment. The only problem was that during the following months, this thought kept coming back again and again. I struggled to make sense of why I couldn't let it go. Clearly, I had to let go of my notion that it was a 'male' comment and get it sorted out. I came up with many reasons why he would say such a thing, but none of them was satisfying. After months of struggling, I came to the realization that this was not something I could do... 'decide not to be sad'... what nonsense!

Choosing not to be sad

And then it happened. I woke up one day a few months later to find that what I had struggled for months to comprehend I now understood completely. I had arrived at a very new place in my grief journey. So I, too, chose not to be sad.

Plan B takes shape

Two significant things happened which assisted me in moving forward with Plan B. One was carefully planned and the other happened quite unexpectedly.

The first was a trip to Vancouver Island to visit a dear friend, followed by four weeks in Australia. I travelled with my sister-in-law and it was a wonderful trip I will always remember.

The second thing was quite spontaneous. I bought a new house three weeks before my trip. While I had been looking at houses to educate myself about prices and locations, I had absolutely no intention of moving for a few years. A friend called one morning to say she and her husband had seen a house for sale they thought I should see. I got out of my pyjamas, drove into Guelph, viewed the house and, with the support of friends and family, bought it. I knew it was the perfect house for me. Before leaving for my trip, the home that Gerald and I had built was put up for sale.

So, this is progress

Having chosen not to be sad doesn't mean that I am never sad anymore. I am sad at times; the difference is that I am not deeply sad all the time. I still cry, but not every day. I still get blindsided by grief, but I no longer live in that space. So, this is progress.

It has become very important to me to 'pay forward' all the love and support I have received in the last two years. One of the ways I have chosen to do this is by becoming a member of the advisory group of the Griefwalk program I attended.

I will participate in training here and in Colorado, which will help me develop skills to help others who are grieving and mourning. Another of my goals is to immerse myself in fibre art and quilting. Perhaps these activities will ignite the spark! Slowly, I am finding purpose in Plan B and I now have hope that, in time, I will find the passion.

The right space, the right place

My home backs on to a green space, which at the moment looks like a winter wonderland. My journey has been one of many small steps. It brought me to many sad, grand, overwhelming, and awe-inspiring insights while on opposite sides of the globe. It eventually brought me to this small, quiet place. As I sit here, slowly growing more comfortable with Plan B, I am grateful for this space, and I am grateful to family and friends for all they have given me. I am in the right place for this moment.

Stopping ensures that when I start again I will be going in the direction that I want. – Peter

The graveyard in my mind

By Mariella Hoy

Overview

I've learned that each fresh grief brings searing memories of previous griefs. I've also concluded that grief comes in two forms: one grief is the trauma of the loss; the other grief is the real sorrow for the loved one.

Our cat died. Lola. I was taken by surprise that we didn't have a few more years together. Twelve years isn't old for a cat. But she got sick and we had to have her euthanized. I loved her. She spent her days curled up on my desk, periodically nudging me as I worked. She slept between my feet at night. A sweet, gentle, loving cat. And very pretty, all black and white, with luminous green eyes. I miss her.

Photo: Alysha Brilla.

What struck me about my grief for her is how wide it swung open the gate to the graveyard in my mind. It brought back memories of burying Maggie, our beautiful black lab. Past cats —Esther, Johnnie, Tiger, and Crusher. Then came memories of my father struggling for breath during his last hours on the hospice bed. And the memory of putting a pair of socks on my mother's cold feet after she died. I hadn't gotten to her bedside in time. These memories, all tightening the already crushing grip around my heart.

Who wants to compound the enormous sadness of one death with memories of all the preceding deaths! No fun. Not fair. Not nice. Close — that — gate!

But isn't it all part of getting older? It comes with the territory. Right? We've lived long enough to have loved many. And to have lost many. I don't know anyone my age who hasn't lost at least one parent, friend, pet, partner, sibling or — chilling thought — child.

The gate latch to the graveyard

The first time the graveyard gate swung open for me was on the last day of work at summer camp, 1979. The campers had left. Out of the blue, I broke down crying. I was suddenly remembering my neighbours who had died the year before. They were part of a family that lived across the courtyard, a family of 13, similar to my own, a family I had once helped my sister to babysit. I remember the phone call from my mother. She said, "Are you sitting down? You should sit down." She proceeded to tell me that five of the 11 children had died, along with their mother. Their house had caught fire, and smoke had billowed up the circular staircase from the basement. I heard later that these five kids were huddled by an upstairs bedroom window, with their 44-year-old mother's arms around them. I remember my stunned incomprehension. Who died? Which ones did she get out the window? Who rolled off the roof into the flowerbed? In which bedroom were they found? I also remember the funeral, and the six white coffins, some of them very small.

My friend at camp asked me, "Don't you think remembering those kids has something to do with the fact that all the campers have just left?"

Ah. The trigger... the gate latch to the graveyard in my mind, where this family's tragedy accounts for six tombstones.

It's a place I don't visit very often, and only when it has been forced upon me by a new grief.

Counting the discounted griefs

It is not only deaths that I bury deep in my memory. I entomb many discounted sorrows, ones often overlooked: a lost pre-term baby, broken relationships, job loss, parenting mistakes, mental health diagnoses of loved ones, the turmoil of my father's last months… all buried in a grieving ground in my mind.

Yesterday, I met a mother whose youngest son recently lost two fingers in an industrial accident. The accident terminated his chosen career path. He's obviously a figure for my sympathy, but I want to acknowledge the suffering she is still experiencing.

Reliving the anguish, not so much the loss

I've come to realize that this graveyard is really the place where I *relive the anguish* that came at the time of the losses, more so than a place where I mourn those who died. I relive the grim realities… having to choose the colour of taffeta for my mother's coffin; having to lower our dog into a hand-dug grave. It is where I relive my violent crying at my mother's funeral, which soaked the shoulder of my bewildered cousin's suit jacket. I relive seeing my big, baby brother overwhelmed by grief. The wait for a diagnosis; the I-have-some-bad-news phone call; the decision made to let them die. These newly experienced, newly learned emotions are powerful and distressing. They are what create the tombstones.

This graveyard, though, isn't where I keep the happy memories of the people and things I loved and lost. Those memories belong to a brighter place, where the sun warms my shoulders and a breeze litters the grass with crabapple blossoms. This place is where I can remember Lola purring in my hammock.

Losses and founds

My inclination is to keep the gate to the painful place closed and locked, unopened until the next loss. Ignoring the graveyard is one way to deal with the pain associated with loss. But I'd rather find some real *value* to these painful memories. What messages are they sending?

I was helped in this by my friend Martin. He was with me the day I took Lola to the vet that final time. A couple of weeks later, he and I had a long talk, over too much coffee, and, although my synapses were misfiring from the caffeine hits, I came away with these thoughts.

As Martin said, the level of pain we have when we lose someone or something is testimony to the value of the attachment. The pain is a sharp reminder of what we hold dear. If we understand what we were so attached to, we can then consciously bring those things into our future life.

For example, what was I attached to in Lola? Sweetness, gentleness, a loving spirit, and beauty. And something to love. So how can I bring those qualities into my future?

What was I attached to in the family members who died in the house fire? Perhaps they represented my own family; the fire could well have been in our house and I could have lost five of my brothers and sisters. So, what am I attached to in my siblings — what are we giving each other? Big-hearted loving, ridiculous humour, intelligent conversation. If I were to lose them, how would I bring those things into my future life?

Becoming soft and malleable

Martin admires people who become soft and malleable as they age, rather than rigid and fixed in their ways. Almost like shape shifters, their softness comes from not holding on too tightly to life's constructs. They learn from their losses and shift shape to recreate a life that accommodates those losses.

I like that idea. By not being rigidly tied to what was, I can be open to what I can become. Like a shape shifter, I can be soft, retaining aspects of what I lost, but in new shapes, in my new life. I can hold onto what I loved about those I lost, but let go of the rest. Maybe that is how the pain of loss can be of value.

I'm hoping that the graveyard may someday become a softer, more peaceful place. I think I'll have to grow more malleable and softer myself, though, before that happens. By which time perhaps I'll have learned to grieve more gently and the tombstones, themselves, will have softened.

Navigating the end of the bend

By Helen
Retired University Professor of English and Women's Studies

> ## Overview
> *Helen has given a good deal of thought to the subject of death. Here she gives us a few perspectives to help us manage our fear of death.*

The appalling snow

Into many a green valley/Drifts the appalling snow. – W.H. Auden

We built our story-and-a-half house as a bungalow basically, with all living possible on the main floor, with wheelchair-width doorways, and with grab bars in the showers. The prospect, though, of someday being unable to climb to the upstairs shower is seriously disheartening.

But death is the real specter, both my death and that of my loved ones. And when I'm hit with sudden terrible glimpses of this prospect, my attempt here at containment feels utterly inadequate. So, this article is not the grand explanation, just current notes from the front.

As I fill in my new day planner, I find that, along with birthdays, I'm entering more new anniversaries of deaths, to support those left behind. My address book too contains little landmines — entries or scratched-out entries for friends and family members who no longer exist.

I have watched the anguish of a friend over the two years since the premature death of her husband. And I buckle at such a future. Death and loss I've identified as triggers for depression, for seeing life as a downward spiral. It doesn't end well, I tell myself.

Notes from the front

She died. She is dead. Is the word so difficult to learn?
– C.S. Lewis, "A Grief Observed"

I've developed three ideas about death, to try to reassure myself. Perhaps it's like leaving the party alone. That interim moment is a lonely one, outside on the dark steps, cut off from the good times, but it's just a transition, and once home, I'm fine alone. The moment itself is hard, not thereafter. ("Home" in this analogy is likely nothingness, but still.)

When my mother was dying, I tried to reassure her and myself by comparing death to falling asleep watching a good television show. The program is gripping, but eventually fatigue wins out, and drifting off is even more compelling.

My third idea is more fanciful and desperate, in the face of annihilation. Perhaps, I tell myself, there'll be no "I" but possibly a "we." Given what physics keeps revealing about connections at subatomic levels, perhaps we join a cosmic dance of atoms and light.

The immensity of the gift

You can't do anything about the length of your life, but you can do something about its width and depth. – H.L. Mencken

I have heartening examples of good lives lived in the shadow of death. My father, recovering in old age from painful hip surgery after walking on a broken hip for five weeks, said, "I haven't reached despair yet." A bit later he exclaimed, at 90, "I don't want to be on a cane for rest of my life!" And wasn't. Even when he had weeks to live, he maintained his equanimity. About his imminent death, I said, "We're going to be very sad," He said, "I won't be there for that," going on to ask whether the birdfeeder he could see was on his neighbour's side of the fence or beyond it.

At a library book sale this fall, I ran into a retired professor of history and asked him how life was going. Despite unspecified "health problems" (he'd had prostate cancer, I knew), he was enjoying writing and grandkids. Gesturing outside, he called on the autumn burst of colour as an image for this life stage. I'd been thinking exactly the same thing and said so with enthusiasm.

Although we have the metaphor of the swan song for a final flourishing, most conceptualizations of aging emphasize deterioration and decrepitude. Yet all around us in this part of the world, nature offers us another model. Never are the trees more glorious.

Nature endures

A society grows great when old men plant trees whose shade they know they shall never sit in. – Greek proverb

So here I stand, horrified at prospects ahead, perhaps more than some people, but scouting about for how to live with aging, bereavement, and eventually dying.

For now, at least, retirement is proving to be a gift. Without the necessity to earn money, which constrained both my time and my choices, and without child-rearing responsibilities, this stage offers me new freedoms. My work and my children were satisfactions of my summer. Now my leaves are turning coral and gold.

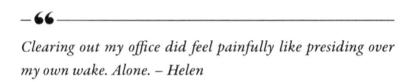

Clearing out my office did feel painfully like presiding over my own wake. Alone. – Helen

❓ Self-Coaching Questions

The fear of death follows from the fear of life. A man who lives fully is prepared to die at any time. – Mark Twain

Confronting Death

When can you set aside time to develop a Plan B in the event that you or your partner are widowed? This plan would include finances, housing, bill payment, funeral arrangements, joint ownership of accounts, legal documents, executors, passwords, contact lists, disposal of personal items, etc.

Can you pinpoint those aspects that you loved most in those you lost? Can you then find ways to bring those aspects into your life in new ways?

What if you were to reserve a place in your heart where you could keep only the happy memories of the people and things you loved and lost, separated as completely as possible from the place where you relive the anguish that came at the time of the losses?

Are there ways that you can grieve more gently?

What if you were to see death as the impetus to live life more vibrantly?

What if you were to choose not to be sad?

Following Frank into retirement:
1 month to go

Money, money, money reprise

Berkeley Breathed, creator of the *Bloom County* comic strip, once described cartoonist techniques that portray emotions. Amongst their weaponry is "sweatles", those drops of sweat projecting from around the head of the cartoon character. "Sweatles" perfectly describes my ongoing thoughts about money and retirement. So, I'm going to try once again to convince myself by the end of this article that I should not be worried about money as retirement looms.

To buy or not to buy, that is the question

Suzanne and I have struggled over the years to find a balance between frugality and rampant consumerism. While we feel that there is no need to replace fraying towels, or chipped and ugly dishes, that does not stop us from lusting after replacements. We can delude ourselves into thinking that we are making the environmentally correct decision by not replacing perfectly serviceable electronics/cars/appliances, but it is really more related to money (much like those hotel room notices that exhort you to save the environment by reusing your towel). Still, thinking twice (or even thrice) before making any purchase is an important concept for us as we head into fixed income retirement. Do we really need it? Will our life be significantly better if we have it? Can the old one be repaired?

Finding money

A colleague and I were discussing cars one evening and we discovered that we shared a common rationale for replacing our cars. We agreed that a car should be kept as long as it is reliable and the annual maintenance is less than the yearly payments on a replacement car. Now, everyone gets a thrill from getting a new car (even if they don't admit it), but just think of the anticipation of waiting a few years before trading in your car. Still not convinced? Then think of the money that you save, which can then be spent on other things.

Besides not purchasing a new car for our retirement, Suzanne and I have also dodged converting our house from oil to propane (I love gas stoves), finding a fridge to match our other appliances (I'm thinking spray paint), upgrading to a new TV to replace our ancient Zenith (nothing good on anyway), and replacing our old washer and dryer (damn things are too easy to fix). Amazingly enough, our life is not appreciably different from not having gotten all that stuff. Furthermore, we are heading into retirement with an extra $40,000 to spend as we need it.

The gilded cage

Unfortunately, like a snake in a garden, money has seduced us into spending because we can afford to spend while we both still have jobs. While we do carefully consider some of our larger purchases, we buy many items without a second thought. It is the loss of this "freedom to spend" that often causes me wakeful nights. I really like to be able to just go out and spend. Continuing to work allows us "freedom to spend" on entertainment, gifts, travel, and our household. In many cases, it also provides health and dental plans, paid vacations, and other perks. However, unless you truly love your work, this comes at the price of less time to enjoy life and the increasing odds that your money will outlive you.

The chicken and the pig

Suzanne and I look upon retirement as a challenge to our resourcefulness — to make do with what we have, while enjoying our life together to the fullest. If the market tanks again, we may have to delay some of our travel plans or the next home renovation. Disappointing, but not devastating. We have busted out of our gilded cage by realizing that money is not the source of our happiness. It can be managed.

Suzanne retires in four days and her job will disappear. I have 33 more work days (I am not counting) and my replacement has been hired. There's an old joke about bacon and eggs: the chicken is involved, but the pig is committed. Oink, oink...

For me, worrying about money has got to be the fiend most foul. How the heck am I supposed to feel comfortable about having enough money for the next 35+ years? – Frank

Reasserting Positive Emotions and a Good Frame of Mind

As we near retirement, and in the first year after retiring, many of us are thrown into a turmoil of mixed emotions: joy, sadness, fear, relief, resistance, grief, surprise, anger, and anxiety. How can we get a grip, reassert positive emotions, and establish a good frame of mind?

The attitude we choose is likely the most influential factor in determining our well-being in retirement.

I struggle with an attitude of caution. I emerge from my cave most days scanning the world for dangers. I shoot down ideas before they can blossom. I worry.

In retirement, the way we approach life isn't going to suddenly change. No matter what our good intentions, we are the same people. That doesn't mean we *can't* change. It can be the work of a lifetime, but we can improve our attitudes. I certainly hope to become less cautious, more relaxed.

Attitude holds a lot of power. It helps shape what we believe to be the limitations and possibilities for ourselves, and for others. Do we take an optimistic attitude (seeing the glass as half full) or pessimistic attitude (seeing the glass as half empty)? The choice is ours to make.

One person's view on this impressed me. In *Man's Search for Meaning,* Viktor Frankl talked of how the demeaning and life-threatening conditions in concentration camps stripped people of their freedoms. He felt that we have one freedom we can hang onto though: our freedom to choose our own attitude. He saw this in some of the men in the camps, those who would comfort and feed others, in spite of their own deprivations.

I'd like to have an attitude that lets me experience more of the child's world. I'm not suggesting rose-tinted glasses, but wouldn't it be nice to be amazed, to marvel, to go through our days with wide-eyed wonder... before we explain it all away? Or scramble back into our cave?

A child doesn't have our matter-of-fact filters. Life is truly incredible. Startling. When a child sees a bird flutter from a tree, her eyes open wide, her mouth forms an 'O' of astonishment, and she laughs with glee. When fireworks go off, a toddler's heart slams in his small ribcage, and a wail of terror erupts. If a ball rolls in front of a youngster, she charges after it with abandon.

Since we get to choose our attitudes, why not tackle retirement with childlike wonder? By choosing an attitude of curiosity and optimism, and by surrounding ourselves with positive people, we significantly increase our chances of feeling deeply satisfied in life.

My friend and coaching colleague Catherine Miller put it this way, "The sun is always shining even though we cannot see it on a cloudy day. Unlike the weather outside, we can change the weather inside."

One of the newsletter contributors, Barb Carriere, chose to see the glass half full. In this quotation, she touches on the notion of abandoned joy:

> *The joy of getting older is much greater self-confidence. It's the loss of angst about what people think of you. It's not arrogance but an understanding of who you are and no longer feeling the need to 'fit in.' I was gardening while in my shorts and pink rubber boots after the rain last week. Didn't matter to me; I was involved in what makes me happy.*

In this chapter are stories from and about people who retired and chose positive attitudes to move them through their retirement days.

- *Oh, the places you'll go! ...with a nod to Dr. Seuss*
- *Where there are toasted tomato sandwiches, there is hope*
- *Liver and onion Wednesdays*
- *When my work ended abruptly, I was catapulted into serious soul searching*
- *What to put on a bucket list*
- *Self-coaching questions*

Oh, the places you'll go! …with a nod to Dr. Seuss

Donna McCaw
Retired High School Teacher

Overview

Donna is a woman who tested her mettle when she retired, who chose adventure — in spite of a chronic health condition that once threatened her life. She explored her passions with curiosity and positivity, travelling the world on her own, and creating a new life path.

I retired at age 54 because I could. I was a high school teacher who had started teaching at age 21 and had reached the 85-factor. I had gone to the retirement planning sessions offered by the Ontario Secondary School Teachers' Federation, explored — intellectually — the option to retire, and was feeling a bit burned out. Teaching was a full-tilt, passionate, creative career for me, one that demanded all resources to the fore.

I felt ready. My son was attending university, I had renovated to have income from an apartment downstairs, lived a simple lifestyle, knew my financial situation, and felt confident.

I have a chronic health condition that started when I was 27 and nearly took my life when I was 38 years old. A doctor had warned me that I might not make it to retirement. I wanted to prove that wrong! Also, my school would be moving to new premises in the fall and I did not want to spend my summer involved with that move. It would be a daunting task. I felt done and done in, with a health condition hanging over my head like the sword of Damocles.

A colleague in my position decided to work another year to buy a new car. It was a practical move, one that I ignored. Ironically, that summer my car died, along with my fridge and dryer. The money I had set aside for a retirement honeymoon trip was swallowed up in a jiffy.

Oh, the possibilities

I decided to go on two trips anyway. The first was to Nicaragua to help with a build. It was a physical, social, and psychological push that boosted my confidence. One afternoon we passed hundreds of cement blocks to the build site from a truck parked a few blocks away. The little woman next to me stayed out in the hot sun all afternoon hefting steadily. When we finally stopped, I learned she was 82 years old. That stopped me whining about my sore and strained muscles. She is still a role model!

Then I came home, rented my house, booked the flights, and flew to Auckland, New Zealand, where I bought a car on my credit card. I spent three months touring the North and South Islands, visiting friends, working on farms, lounging in hot pools, and discovering another country. Each day was a new adventure and a series of discoveries about the place and about myself. That was the best retirement honeymoon I could have experienced. I pushed myself out of my cocoon comfort zone, challenged myself, and treated each day as a new opportunity.

I lived in campgrounds, cooked for myself often, met new people, saw amazing sights, kept a journal, and realized I could handle this new life of possibilities. I pushed envelopes I had put myself into and increased the space for my experience of a new life full of options, choices, and wonder.

I took a three-week side trip to Bali, Indonesia to meet my sister and her friends. Another culture, more beauty, and appreciation for the richness of life. Then, I spent time on my own in Kuala Lumpur, Malaysia for a few days and coped just fine. My biggest fear was dealing with a health issue on my own, but the sword of Damocles did not fall. I could do it. I could tackle this new life of whatever retirement had in store.

Photo: Brian A Jackson, Shutterstock.com.

This four-month trip became the microcosm of the new life I was heading for now. A bit of this, a bit of that, while following my heart, my curiosity, and sharing with like-minded, positive people. I would find a great bottle of wine, some cheese and chocolate, and have a campground picnic with fellow travellers. I tried new experiences, like working on organic farms, haunting libraries, museums, and movie theatres on rainy days, hiking, climbing, swimming, and stopping to watch the sea lions — and breathing in ocean air. Stretching, reaching, relaxing enough to listen to the inner wise voice, and pay attention to the new rhythm of body and mind. This trip was the coming out of the cocoon of my old life with an inviting vision of a new one.

The waiting place

I got back both pumped and exhausted. I started looking for a project. How about tutoring? It turned out to not be as inspiring as I had anticipated. Teaching abroad? I did not want to sign a two-year contract. I took courses, attended lectures, worked in the forlorn garden, started a fitness regimen, volunteered for community groups, did storytelling, and waited for the next place for my time and energy.

The next adventure

My sister provided my next adventure by choosing to leave nursing in California to return to Canada, but British Columbia this time. We bought a house together there.

I flew to Santa Barbara, helped pack her car and rented trailer, and enjoyed goodbye parties and garage sales. We drove up the stunning coasts of California, Oregon, and Washington to the ferry that took us to Victoria. We started ripping up carpet the afternoon the property closed. We sanded, replaced drywall, removed wallpaper, cleaned, painted, hired workmen, started a garden, and tore around to garage and yard sales. Room by room, we worked our way through the house.

We then rented some rooms to students who were coming to learn English. I cleaned, shopped, and cooked, while my sister went back to work. The English teacher/cook came in handy for tutoring and conversation.

Like my sister before me, I fell in love with the West Coast. So, when she bought me out of our partnership, I bought a condo. Although I've rented it out for now, I crave the treat of cherry blossoms in February! I have since read Lyndsay Green's *The Perfect Home for a Long Life* and see more of the West Coast in my future.

Reflecting on the journey

That first summer was a long exhale, a sense of liberation, and a growing sense of excitement about new experiences. The first fall was a string of relaxed Sunday evenings knowing I would not be back at work on Monday. The long honeymoon trip took me to new realities a long way from my old routines and demands. The house in B.C. was the reorientation project that got me on a new path in a new place.

On returning to Ontario, I found new purpose in teaching courses, founding a biannual literary event, volunteering, writing a book, and starting a small business. I found a structure that works for me, and outlets for my interests, passions and values. I have new communities in both provinces. I feel blessed and grateful for the experiences I've had and look forward to what comes next.

Oh, and the places I've been since? Italy, Spain, France, Ireland, Scotland, India three times, Argentina, Chile, Turkey, Newfoundland, New Brunswick, Nova Scotia, Prince Edward Island, Quebec, Alberta, Washington State, Florida, Mexico, Australia, and back to New Zealand.

Rather than analyzing life, I'm trying to be there. Rather than being afraid of what is next, I am flinging myself forward into the fray with no particular goal in mind. – Fiona

Where there are toasted tomato sandwiches, there is hope

By Brad Morley
Retired High School English Teacher

Overview

The delights of toasted tomato sandwiches and an attitude of accepting the unpredictable have carried Brad through the aggravations of aging. He chose to embrace the possible and to marvel at the simplest things. And hungry groundhogs be damned!

In a delightful coincidence of events, my first Saturday in August started with a toasted tomato sandwich. On the night before, we were finally able to have a good friend from university days over to dinner after many years of not seeing him. His name is Laz and he's a lawyer. More often than not, talk of or with Laz over the thirty-five years since graduation conjured memories of the toasted tomato sandwiches he would make for a select few of us in residence at U of T. Always in the fall, always after he'd been home to the farming country near Delhi, Ontario, and always with freshly picked tomatoes he'd brought back. Good bread toasted, a generous swipe of mayo, two or three thick slices of the red beefsteak variety, a few good dashes of black pepper, and there before us a simple feast of absolute delight. Such is the power of friendship and food that to this day these sandwiches remain one of my happiest memories of what was a quite wonderful period in my life.

And so, with last night's dinner, wine, conversation, and laughter still resonating, I headed out — coffee in hand — for my morning stroll through our flower and vegetable patches. Somewhat hidden under a broad expanse of coneflower leaves, the first of my "Early Girl" tomatoes hung, reddened and ruined, having fallen prey to the hungry groundhog that has tormented me and a few select plants off and on over the past several weeks. I picked it anyway and discovered two thirds of it was in perfect order.

I decided that my first toasted tomato sandwich of the season was the best way to put this fruit to good use and to get the last laugh, for now at least, on my gnawing pest. I also took added delight in the seasonal coincidence of dinner with Laz, memories of residence life, and the immediacy of what looks to be a long and fruitful harvest, large rodents notwithstanding.

Rodents notwithstanding

The dominant themes of retirement life for me can be summed up with this little anecdote of Laz and the early tomatoes: remembering the past can make the present even richer, old connections may well be restored, what appears disappointing at first can lead to better things, careful cultivation today can result in rewards worth waiting for, and (at the risk of even more cliché) the simplest pleasures can involve enjoyable multi-layered experiences.

Now, I am not foolish enough to believe my garden-dinner-sandwich metaphor provides the sum of all retirement's parts. I could, for instance, bring in my poor Asian lilies' struggles with the voracious red lily beetle, my grapevine's battle with the sluggish but persistent Japanese beetle, and my frustration over the viburnum beetles' devastation of the enormous snowball bush by our driveway. But I won't — other than to say that the pleasures provided by all that is in our front and back gardens far outweigh the relatively minor aggravations created by a few pests.

Retirement — both less and more

Similarly, the debilitating vertigo that played havoc for eight months with the first year of my wife and me being retired together, the abscessed molar and resulting double root canal I endured, the oh-so-slow-to-heal strained hamstring that kiboshed my running program for ten months — these things and more have made retirement less than it could have been. But set in the scale against our three October weeks in Italy; our moving to a new house in an old town (or is that an old house — 1895 — in a new town, Guelph?); the hours and hours of rewarding reading; our new lunchtime ritual of working out the Globe and Mail's cryptic crossword, an exercise which in itself is a metaphor worth exploring; and so on; the suffering and frustration retired life has thrown at me is scant concern in relation to the pleasure and wonder that the changes afforded by retirement have wrought.

Acknowledging luck

Not everyone will be as lucky as I, once working life wanes and retirement... What is the best word for this space? Looms? Beckons? The more neutral Awaits? Which one occurs most fitting to you? For me, even though I really enjoyed my 32 years teaching, retirement has been, on the whole, brilliant. But I have a good pension which makes for an easier time than many will experience. I have a partner and good friends with whom I quite enjoy spending time. No doubt, I have had luck on my side. But perhaps I have been luckiest in having inherited from my mother an ability to enjoy and even to marvel at so many of the simplest things: purple coneflowers in the sun, chipmunks cavorting in the grass, the two-thirds good bits of an otherwise ruined tomato.

Can't afford the luxury of not being hopeful

It is almost impossible to avoid metaphor and cliché when writing about retirement, what it's like, how best to prepare for it, and how best to live it. While it is very important to have the nuts and bolts of certain preparatory things fitted well in place before retirement begins, one should also keep an open mind, express a willingness to accept the unpredictable, and embrace the possible.

An old friend told me years ago that he lives his life by the metaphor of hidden treasure turning up everywhere and in all things. Another friend, preparing for a year away from work, responded to my comment about his year off by saying he was planning a year on. This subtle shift in language underscored a significant difference in his way of seeing the future from my way.

A few days ago, a Detroit resident being interviewed on radio about the recent problems caused by the city shutting off the water supply to many of its poorest citizens had a wonderful response to the reporter's question about the future for this resident and her family of five children: "I can't afford the luxury of not being hopeful," she said. I had to repeat this to myself a couple of times to more fully understand it, and then I was struck by her wisdom and insight. What a constructive attitude, I thought. What a sensible way to look at things. I'd wager she'd know what to do with retirement were she ever to be granted that benefit. She'd know what to do with that damned groundhog and those damaged tomatoes.

What I've been able to figure out so far, since retiring, is to breathe. – Joan

Liver and onion Wednesdays

By Mariella Hoy

Overview

A positive frame of mind, resilience, and a Kubota lawn mower were all that were needed by this old man in his quest for a meal of liver and onions.

He drove up and parked his orange Kubota lawn mower near the restaurant entrance, a restaurant in a has-been gas station in the middle of farm country. After tilting up the seat to protect it in the event of rain, he made his way slowly into the restaurant and sat down at a table.

He seemed to be on the older side of old, maybe 90 years old. He removed his grey train engineer's cap, planted a cane firmly between his feet, and, leaning forward, let it take his weight. His high-top runners were open at the laces, perhaps to relieve swelling in his feet, perhaps because he couldn't bend over to lace them up.

The lure

What brought him all this way in the fading light? Did he drive the lawn mower because he no longer had a driver's license? Bad eyesight? A stroke? Or could he no longer afford a car now that his fixed income had dwindled in old age?

After catching his breath, he said to the waitress, "Liver and onions." Raising his hand in a peace symbol, he added, "Two pieces."

The day was Wednesday — Liver and Onions Day at the restaurant. Their best cook makes a point of being there on Wednesday. He knows how easy it is to ruin liver.

Creative, resourceful, and whole

I'm always struck by the ingenuity and creativeness that people bring to bear when they want something and have run into an obstacle. In coach training, I was taught that people are creative, resourceful, and whole, and I've certainly seen this again and again. I've learned never to give anyone a solution to their problem — they will find a solution and it will be better than anything I could propose.

This guy at the restaurant wanted liver and onions and had no way of getting it. His ingenuity led him to the lawn mower, which brought him to the restaurant, which prepared him liver and onions. Two portions. He found a way.

Finding a way

Finding a way in retirement is similar. Whatever obstacles we're facing, isn't it really about trusting that we will find a way?

Retirement life is not about looking for a fantasy meal that no restaurant can create — this keeps us in the world of dreaming. Nor is it about accepting the bread-and-butter meal of the status quo — this keeps us in the world of safety and boredom. The trick is to find that truly delightful meal we're craving — one that we know is out there somewhere — and then to make sure we find a way to get to the restaurant, on a lawn mower or whatever it takes.

Unexpected dishes

We won't always be served the dish we expect. If we trust ourselves, however, we will find a way to get what we need. And whatever dish is served up, we can count on it being one hell of an adventure.

The trick is to find that truly delightful meal we're craving.
– Mariella

When work ended abruptly, I was catapulted into serious soul searching

By Martin

Overview

Sometimes retirement sends us questing for answers to the big-picture questions, as it did for Martin, whose transition into retirement was difficult, due to a chronic health condition and an identity entwined with his work.

I haven't officially retired but I haven't worked in years. I was there, at my job — and then (like the skunk I just watched disappear into a hedge) — I was gone. There was no retirement party, no pithy moment of realizing: "This is it, the last time I set foot in this place!"

I have a chronic condition that allows me to be energetic for only short periods of time. For a while I thought I'd be able to return to work; that hasn't happened. As I found out, there are a lot of us who didn't plan on ending our career; it just ended. Often our identity is so entwined with our work that to have it end unexpectedly can be hard.

The Endlessly Changing Sky

After a decidedly difficult and awkward transition period, I was able to start enjoying the sheer pleasure of time-without-time-constraints. Delightful moments have grown out of a less hurried life. For example, I love spending time on our deck with the huge maple that hugs our house. I revel in the endlessly changing sky.

I am very lucky. There are many pleasures, like spontaneously having coffee with a friend, taking time to play the piano, whipping a super ball around the kitchen while trying not to break things! I have unscripted time to spend with family, for day-to-day tasks, and for special interests.

The Big Picture Stuff

When my career ended in an abrupt, tumultuous way, I was catapulted into serious soul searching. Looking back, I see that the way I adapted was by throwing myself into grappling with the big picture questions. There were many things I wanted to know. What is the relationship of the mind to the self? How do we deal with suffering and darkness? Is this reality that we experience the only reality? Is unconditional happiness possible? What do I want my future to be?

So many questions... This was not an intellectual exercise; I genuinely sought, and needed, answers! Family and friends were a great help. I also sought guidance through spiritual ceremonies, meditation retreats, and modern western therapies, and so spent many hours engaged in these activities.

My interest in big picture questions and answers, which my wife rightly calls my "quest," started long ago and intensified after I left work. The "quest" had no specific destination, but had to do with wanting to feel more deeply connected, more at home in my skin, in the world and in the universe.

The Great Mystery

What if I hadn't ended my career the way I did? Would I be a significantly different person now? Hard to say, but, when my career ended, I was pushed to further acknowledge the Great Mystery. I love that expression, "the Great Mystery," which is a term used by this continent's First Peoples. To me, "Great" conveys the sense of awe that I had as a child and that I continue to feel at times. "Mystery" implies that it's normal to want to figure out how I fit into the big picture. It's natural to be confused and it's okay to stumble and guess. Humility is in order in this vast, largely uncharted territory.

Since I stopped work, experiences have taught me to let go of fears, to discover more deeply the power of love, to trust others, make friends, and feel the strength there is in community. I am more able to see and accept my blind spots with compassion and to make changes. I can let go of some notions I held onto way past their expiry date. I am learning to follow my heart.

It's been a great ride since I got to dabble and dive into the Great Mystery and what a positive difference it has made. The difficult transition from work and my former identity to whoever it is I am now has led to valuable insights into the nature of things.

I am more able to see and accept my blind spots with compassion and to make changes. I can let go of some notions I held onto way past their expiry date. – Martin

What to put on a bucket list

Mariella Hoy

Overview

Not having a bucket list myself, I looked into the value of having one and concluded that it keeps us hunting for ways to enrich our lives with good things.

If you haven't heard the first speech made in the movie *The Bucket List,* you should watch the movie just to savour those words. The character Carter Chambers (played by Morgan Freeman) talks of his friend Edward Cole (played by Jack Nicholson), a cranky billionaire who owns the hospital in which they have both been diagnosed with terminal lung cancer. They share a room, and their journeys toward death. Carter tells us that you can measure yourself in life by the people who measure themselves by you. He goes on to tell us that Edward packed more living into his last days than most of us do in a lifetime.

When it becomes evident that they will both soon die, they start a bucket list, a list of things they'd like to do before they 'kick the bucket.'

What is worthy of the list?

The aspect of the movie that interests me is what they chose to put on their list. I've never had a bucket list and sometimes wonder if I lack imagination. Imagination fuels what is possible, after all. At other times, I pat myself on the back, telling myself complacently that I don't need a bucket list because I already have the important things in my life. But I do wonder if a list might spur me forward in life somehow, and so am interested in what's on people's bucket lists.

Carter and Edward's bucket list, as best as I can determine, includes the following:

- Witness something truly majestic
- Help a complete stranger for a common good
- Laugh 'til I cry
- Drive a Shelby Mustang
- Kiss the most beautiful girl in the world
- Get a tattoo
- Skydive
- Visit Stonehenge

- Spend a week at the Louvre
- See Rome
- Dine at La Cherie d'Or
- See the Pyramids, Hong Kong, Victoria Falls, and Serengeti
- Ride the Great Wall of China

They tackle the list, crossing things off as they go, and adding more. They fly over the North Pole, go on a lion safari in Tanzania, attempt to see Mount Everest, and visit the Taj Mahal. After gallivanting around the world, Carter comes to a better understanding and appreciation of his love for his wife. In an attempt to influence Edward to find a similar happiness, Carter poses two questions. He says these are questions the gods at the gates of heaven ask the dead:

1. Have you found joy in your life?

2. Has your life brought joy to others?

In the end, what brings Carter and Edward real joy, and what is most meaningful to them, is revitalization of their special relationships — for Carter, with his wife, and for Edward, with his estranged daughter. And Edward kisses his granddaughter for the first time, realizing he is kissing the most beautiful girl in the world.

The Chewbacca principle

One item on Carter and Edward's list that I would add to mine is "Laugh 'til I cry." This finally happens for the characters in the movie when Carter reveals that Edward's beloved Kopi Luwak coffee is processed through the digestive track of a breed of wild tree cat, giving the coffee the distinct aroma of its gastric juices. Edward says, "You're shitting me!" Without missing a beat, Carter replies, "Cats beat me to it!"

I recently saw a Facebook video that made me laugh like that. Maybe you've seen it: *Laughing Chewbacca Mask Lady*.[1] When it was released in 2016, 104 million people viewed it in only three days. Candace Payne videotaped herself opening a birthday gift, a Star Wars Chewbacca mask that makes the creature's trademark noise. Throughout her video, Candace reveals a pure, open enjoyment of her new toy. Having ramped up to tear-producing laughter, she signs off with the statement, "It's the simple joys." Too true!

---

1 Deak, J. (2016, May 9). *Laughing Chewbacca Mask Lady* [video]. YouTube. https://youtu.be/y3yRv5Jg5TI

Going for good feelings

On any bucket list, positive emotions are definitely worth pursuing: laughter, joy, love, gratitude, hope, and contentment. I believe these are at the root of what motivates us. But what about those times when we can't generate positive emotions — the situation is perilous; we've been dealt crummy cards. Are we prepared for those times? Have we cultivated a Zen-like ability to accept what is, to play the cards we're dealt? Maybe our bucket list helps in these situations by drawing our attention away from the tough stuff.

And how does all this relate to retirement? Retirement is a time for rebuilding the scaffolding of our lives. We have a window of opportunity to set new habits in place. Will these habits include time to reflect on what makes our lives meaningful? I'm noticing that many retired people are very busy... doing, doing, doing. Is it just empty busyness? I'm hoping not; I'm hoping that all this doing is helping people find ways to feel valued and loved, helping them build new identities in retirement, and helping them discover real meaning in their lives. And good feelings.

Measuring!

In the opening lines of *The Bucket List,* Carter says, "Me, I believe you measure yourself by the people who measure themselves by you." It would be good to think I could have a positive impact on others and the way they think and act after I'm long gone. However, I can't fully support the notion of measuring ourselves. I'm tired of measuring and being measured. In fact, if I put anything besides "Laugh 'til I cry" on my bucket list, it might be a wish to stop measuring and judging myself and others. Wouldn't that be a great way to live... accepting ourselves, accepting others?

Shopping for delight

The real value of a bucket list, in my view, is that it keeps us hunting for ways to enrich our lives with good things. It keeps us focused on positives, and less so on all that is bugging us.

Carter and Edward travel the world celebrating their lives and searching for meaning. In the end, the highlights of their bucket list are their renewed relationships. Also, they come to see that they have 'helped a complete stranger for a common good' — each other — through their shared experience and by coming to know and love each other. Their bucket list is the catalyst for the happiness they create for themselves.

So... great relationships, good feelings, and laughing 'til you cry. I love the notion that we can go shopping for delight. It's there for us if we look, and I think perhaps it helps to name it on a bucket list.

—❝—

About the time we were preparing to move to this retirement community, and dealing with losses in health, thinking about deaths and griefs of different kinds, a wise woman said to me, "there's lots of letting go" in this stage of life. And there is.
– Ann

—❞—

Self-Coaching Questions

If you change the way you look at things, the things you look at change.
– Wayne Dyer

Reasserting positive emotions and a good frame of mind — Getting your head on straight about retirement

What attitude would you like to choose in retirement? What attitude needs the boot?

When you put things on your bucket list and then cross them off, do you examine whether they brought you the rewards you anticipated?

When you look at your bucket list, can you see ways in which you measure and judge yourself and others? What are you still measuring that doesn't need measuring?

If you're not getting what you hoped for in retirement, how can you make sure it's still one hell of an adventure?

Are you filling your life with activities that provide meaning and joy? Are you shopping for delight? What does delight look like to you?

Following Frank into Retirement: This is it! 14 days to go.

The luxury of being

I have 14 working days left before my retirement. A good contact with whom I have worked over the years called me up about doing some consulting in January and February. The work was very similar to my current work and one of the reasons that I'm retiring at age 58 instead of 60 plus. After some sober reflection, I decided that I did not have to do it because I did not want to do it. I thanked him for thinking of me and declined the opportunity. Ahhhhh!

Taking a bow

My company has hired an excellent person to take over my position and my remaining work time is booked with him to ensure a smooth transition between us. Travelling with him has been interesting, in that as he is slowly getting weighed down by my responsibilities, I'm feeling lighter with each passing day.

I've also made my last trip to the head office and said farewells to my many friends and colleagues there. Even though my company drives me crazy, I will miss all the great people. The group I directly work with even banded together and bought me the perfect farewell gift. Bagpipes! It feels great to be truly appreciated.

Bagpipes – 1, Frank – 0

Besides a quick honk in my hotel room, I didn't get a chance to try the pipes out until I got home three days later. It quickly became clear that in the intervening nine years since I last played the pipes I had lost a lot of technique and lip muscle. There were also a million and one things to learn about maintaining my own pipes. I was a little stressed because there wasn't enough time to practise and the new reeds that I needed would not arrive for a couple of weeks. That is until I realized that the reeds will arrive in time for my retirement and I will have lots of time to practise. At least, when I start playing on my deck, the neighbours will have the benefit of all my practice over the winter.

Expand-a-plan

We had a fun party three weeks ago for Suzanne's retirement/60th birthday. Friends, neighbours, and relatives all came together for some karaoke and appetizers. Suzanne felt that we should also celebrate my retirement in some way. I'm not big on parties so we've decided to go to Quebec City for a few days and stay one night in the ice hotel there. Since we're headed out that way, we'll see if we can visit friends in Toronto, our son and his fiancée in Ottawa, and Suzanne's brother and wife in Drummondville. On our return to Toronto, we may hop on a plane south, if we find a cheap enough last-minute package, or we may drop in to see our daughter and her partner in Peterborough. Or both. We get to make our plans as we go. What a luxury.

Stay tuned...

It wouldn't be fair to paint a completely rosy picture of my upcoming retirement without mentioning that I'm still quite concerned about finding time heavy on my hands. I've depended on work to fill most of the hours of my weeks. I get antsy if I'm not doing something constructive. Even last Saturday evening, after a very full week of work travel, I found myself at loose ends. This time I was saved by needing to write this article for Mariella's newsletter. That in itself was a bit of a revelation, in that there is no reason why I couldn't continue writing since it has been enjoyable sharing my thoughts as they bubble up to the surface. I could also try writing something else — it has been probably about half a century since I last did any creative writing (except for funding proposals).

So, if you're interested, don't touch that dial! I'm only too happy to share the angst and joy as my journey into retirement moves into the next phase. Thanks for sticking with me so far.

7 Finding Meaning and Well-Being in Retirement

After my devastation and withdrawal from the battlefield at the toxic job I had years ago, I forged a new 'career' for myself. In a way, it was retirement for me; I was doing what I loved, whether or not I was paid for it. And I could imagine doing so into my old age. As a life coach, I was now working with people intent on creating purpose, passion, and well-being in their lives.

I can't describe my new work as anything other than euphoric. To be delving into the mystery of what makes people happy, to be co-exploring the question of what changes are needed to move to a better place in life, this work fed me. No longer did I feel an undercurrent of unrest. Meaning and purpose fueled me.

I was back to those three questions that fascinated me from when I was a kid:

1. What do you want to be when you grow up?
2. What makes you happy?
3. What changes do you want to make to create a better life for yourself?

These questions loom large in the minds of those considering retirement and those newly retired.

In this chapter, you'll find a selection of stories and thoughts that delve into this juicy subject:

- *I'm fine. Really.*
- *In search of the meaning of life (still)*
- *Retirement — a time for small things*
- *Leaving behind a life legacy that goes beyond ego*
- *Self-coaching questions*

... doing something 'worthwhile' has to me the taste of duty and conscience. Not my favourite flavour combination by a long shot... – Frank

I'm fine. Really.

By Anson Laytner
Retired Interreligious Initiative Program Manager,
School of Theology & Ministry, Seattle University

Overview

Anson had a retirement plan in place and all was going well... until a few serious wrinkles disturbed his serenity.

I had retirement all figured out; my schedule was set: Get up early at 5ish to read the paper. Wake Richelle, my wife, at 6:15 and do yoga together. Make breakfast, pack her lunch, and push her out the door to catch the bus for work. Go to my home office and write or do research until noon. Eat lunch. Take a nap. Walk to the grocery store or somewhere else to get some exercise. Come home and make dinner. Spend the evening with Richelle, watching TV or going for a walk or exercising at the gym. In bed by 11 pm at the latest — if I haven't fallen asleep before then.

First some background: The university at which I worked gave me the impetus to retire when major funding for my program ran out and new funding had not been found. I was asked to switch to half-time. Working half-time made me realize two things: first, that I could survive on what I was earning, which was about the same as I'd receive in social security benefits; and second, that the part-time position was nowhere near as fulfilling as the full-time position had been. I concluded that I might as well do what I really want to do, so I took a leap of faith and retired.

What I hadn't counted on was inertia, and guilt, and loneliness, and loss of status, and financial anxiety. But other than this, I'm doing great. Seriously. Let me tell you why.

Finances

The evidence notwithstanding, I still have financial anxiety every time an unanticipated expense pops up. But slowly I am realizing that as long as the economy is doing well, we'll be fine too. And even if it tanks for a while, it will recover at some point and so will our finances. And if an economic disaster were to happen, it would put many other people in the same dire straits as us, so why worry. In other words, my anxiety is manageable.

Status

In my working life, I was a major player in Seattle's interfaith scene, and working at Seattle University's School of Theology and Ministry put me at the center of much of it. I was surprised at how quickly I became irrelevant when I retired! What a blow to my ego — it was a revelation and an intimation of mortality too. But it made me realize that if I want to continue to do interfaith work, it will be as a volunteer and whatever I accomplish or contribute will be on my own, without an institution's prestige backing me up.

Loneliness

A cat is a good companion but a lousy conversationalist and I quickly realized that I had to look elsewhere to meet this need. So, until Richelle retires and I can pester her 24/7, I make lunch or happy-hour dates with friends and colleagues. Some days, however, I must admit to feeling lonely and missing the camaraderie of my office mates.

Guilt

This brings me to guilt. I have retiree's guilt. I look younger than I am and I am in pretty good health, so I think I still ought to be working, especially when I see people who look older than I still working. I feel I owe the world an explanation — except that I really don't — and so I tell myself, repeatedly, to just get over it. And that works, repeatedly.

Inertia

Inertia. Probably my biggest issue. "Inertia" — a property of matter in which it continues in a state of rest until acted upon by an external force. As applied to retirement, it translates as self-motivation and the absence of deadlines. I thought I had this covered. To begin with, I had commitments to write several major academic articles and, when these are done, I have a manuscript just waiting to be finished and ideas for several more books just waiting to be researched. Not to mention that I edit a website, publish a newsletter and have daily correspondence to attend to. And enough chores to label me a househusband.

So, what do I do? When Richelle leaves for work, I wander around the house, or play with Cat, or surf the Internet, or play solitaire, generally doing everything I can to avoid and evade doing something constructive. I always thought I was self-motivated and now, to my surprise, I seem to have become a sluggard. Sometimes it can take me up to several hours to settle down. Sometimes I never get down to it. Is this okay? Am I really allowed to just do nothing?

The freedom to do nothing. Is this what retirement is really about? But if I do nothing, where do I find the meaning in my life? Work used to take up so much time and energy, but it did provide purpose. It had meaning and I enjoyed it most of the time. But now? Is what I do now of any value or am I just marking time until you-know-what happens?

Such questions! Thank God I told Mariella that I would write this article and have a deadline to meet! And now that it's done, I'm off to lunch...

66

What I hadn't counted on was inertia, and guilt, and loneliness, and loss of status, and financial anxiety. But other than this, I'm doing great. Seriously. – Anson

99

In search of the meaning of life (still)

By Rose Morley
Retired Elementary School Teacher

Overview

What happens when, a year and a half into retirement, you're still experimenting and feeling your way, not quite sure what gives you a sense of purpose, or what counts as worthwhile in your days. These are the queries that unsettle Rose.

A former teaching colleague who recently retired emailed me with a brimming litany of what she has been up to, expressing her amazement at — and difficulty understanding — people who feel a sense of loss or worthlessness once they have retired. And then the final salvo, "Sad, really."

Hmm. And I actually thought I was doing all right. I'd been feeling my way through this new life, not quite sorting it out yet and, yes, still having days wondering what I had accomplished. Now it seems I am a pathetic creature because I am still searching, still experimenting. And what happened to all those pursuits I dreamed about while I tortured myself over whether to give a nine-year-old the benefit of the doubt because it is hard to read the degree delineations on a scuffed and ancient protractor? Why had I not jumped whole-heartedly into retirement and never looked back? Why, eighteen months later, do I find myself taking a stress management course at the local university? What do I have to be stressed about? I'm retired, for God's sake!

I find myself listening to this tune often, mostly against my will. The earworm of guilt, planted by a perfectly innocent communiqué from someone who just recently joined the ranks of the retired. The burden has been lifted! Hallelujah! A new adventure awaits! So what the hell is wrong with you?

A pursuer of solitary activities

So here I am, a year and a half later, still wondering, questioning, examining, discarding, refining. While the great majority of my retired friends are joiners of choirs, theatre groups, book clubs and exercise classes, I am essentially a pursuer of solitary activities — not just solo acts, but ones which happen to require self-discipline and only intermittent social contact. And in spite of wanting (mostly very fervently) to be involved in these activities, I find myself still trying to adjust to a world with no colleagues, nothing to complain about on a Friday afternoon in a pub, and without the signposts that ensure you are a contributing cog in a wheel that carries you through the world, assuring you that you are part of that world.

I confess I was one of those overly earnest children who wept on days when I had to stay home from school, sick. I had an overwhelming sense that the world was continuing without me, that I was being left behind; even the sounds of children shouting to one another as they walked home from school would bring on a fresh bout of tears.

What did I get done today?

Now I have stepped into a world where, if you are not a cog in a wheel, your very existence is questioned, albeit tactfully, at a dinner party, or simply disregarded by those who are so busy they don't have time to be sick. When I encounter another new retiree, I am immediately regaled with tales of how busy he/she is. It never occurs to him/her to, well, pose that question of accountability: what did I get done today?

I am discovering that retirees, like Tolstoy's unhappy families, are all different. Sound like a bit of a "duh" realization? In reality, when we encounter one another, there are certain accepted beliefs and assumptions about retirement — unfettered freedom, losing track of what day it is, adventure, and fulfilling goals and ambitions which we may never have been even dimly aware of during our working life, but which are suddenly clear and urgent. Oh yes, retirement can be/should be all of that.[1]

The weight of being your own boss

But like those students, sometimes you don't know what else retirement can bring. Just as the employment gremlins (real and/or imagined) have released their grasp on you, you are handed the control yourself and, whoa, what a responsibility it is! If you have been in the habit of operating reasonably well within a set of parameters, you sometimes get very used to working within the box. Suddenly the sides of the box are flattened and it is all up to you. It takes a while to be the boss when you haven't been for a very long time (at least not since you were a child and believed no one was the boss of you). Both heady and weighty.

---

1 And much more, as my intermediate English students used to add when they ran out of details but wished to indicate that they were actually fully cognitive that there were more ideas brewing up there in their heads but proper essay writing style forbids the run-on.

Maybe I'm a slow learner. Maybe it's my personality (as suggested by my cello teacher, rather stymied by my too intense approach to learning a new instrument), or maybe it is just all about the process of figuring it out and never quite doing so.

Exchanging cash for time

I find metaphors somewhat comforting — to describe, live by, endure. When I retired, like anyone else I had to consider the reality of a reduced income. I blithely told myself I was now exchanging cash for time — the new currency now an embarrassment of riches. Wow, look at it all! I could just dip my fingers through it and luxuriate in it, which meant that I could spend hours on the Globe cryptic crossword and not bother washing my face until noon.

But soon enough my need for routine and ritual prevailed, as well as my anal compulsion to cross off tasks listed in a little datebook (yes, I still keep one — vestiges of a career in education). You have to know you have done something with your day and washing your face doesn't count.

How we spend our days is how we spend our lives

I listened and noticed. I continue to rise early in the morning because I love to watch for the moment when enough light has emerged in the sky to call it day; because I savour the quiet of the house when I am the only one awake; because it has become an absolute essential to take advantage of the fleeting opportunity to write when nothing has been allowed to be imprinted on my brain quite yet. Read the paper, put the kettle on, get dressed — I'll have lost it.

Annie Dillard, who famously said "How we spend our days is how we spend our lives," offers up another way to regard the passage of time in retirement, a process that is both too fast and too slow. What I do daily — half-finished, half-formed, just beginning, new or familiar — adds up. When I am absorbed and totally given to whatever I am doing, it is glorious and there is no deeper satisfaction. When I walk a little away from it, I can see how it becomes me, how it is both the character of my life and the character of me.

The abundance of tomorrows

It can be useful to ask on a daily basis, how will I spend this day? There are times at day's end when I am dismayed because I have knitted a sock twice, only to find some grievous error just before bed or that there was nothing but blather on the page today; yet, for no reason at all, I am given another abundance tomorrow.

Admittedly, I was not much good during my work life at putting faith in the following day, but in retirement you get to realize that it is mostly up to you, both a blessing and a curse, perhaps. After you are fed, watered and warmed, it's all on you. Learning how to spend your newfound currency (which keeps coming to you, unbidden, at least for a little while) is tricky, but you might finally recognize that an afternoon on a couch with a book, with the brilliant winter sun streaming in, is not like washing your face. It counts.

—66————————————————

Why, eighteen months later, do I find myself taking a stress management course at the local university? What do I have to be stressed about? I'm retired, for God's sake! — Rose

————————————————99—

Retirement — a time for small things

By Mariella

Overview

In this article, I play with the idea that retirement is a time for small acts of kindness, small accomplishments, small enjoyments, and small needs.

Retirement is a time for small acts. No longer do we have careers to advance. Competition can be set aside, ego banished. We do not need to impress. We can choose where to excel or whether to excel at all. It is a time to give our stuff away, to pass it on to the next generation. It is our chance to lighten up, to soften up, to become smaller.

Small acts of kindness

Too often we underestimate the power of a touch, a smile, a kind word, a listening ear, an honest compliment, or the smallest act of caring, all of which have the potential to turn a life around. – Leo Buscaglia

In retirement we can slow down and take care how we spend the moments of our day. Given this wealth of time, our small, kind selves now have a stage on which to flourish. We can gleefully plan small acts of kindness. We can spontaneously give, without expectation of receiving in return.

These kindnesses that come from the heart give us great pleasure, and are so good to receive.

From retired friends I recently received a hand-knit infinity scarf, help moving furniture, a compliment, and a freshly brewed cup of coffee that came with a rejuvenating chat.

Small accomplishments

Great things are done by a series of small things brought together.
– Vincent Van Gogh

In retirement, we can savour the process of doing... replacing a light switch, turning soil over in the garden, gently wiping a child's nose. We can absorb ourselves in the act of doing, without being attached to the end result... with no person, system, or organization pressuring us to do it in a prescribed way or demanding a particular result.

We can embrace imperfection, as I have with the small musings in this piece of writing.

Or we can choose to seek perfection. I have two brothers-in-law who are striving to perfect baked goods. One is working on the perfect oatmeal chocolate chip cookie. He has made them dozens of times, each time changing the spicing — a little more ginger, a little less nutmeg — or changing the cooking time — 10 seconds more or 30 seconds less. The cherry pie and old-fashioned white bread are the endeavours of another brother-in-law. He counts the number of pulses on the blender when making the pie crust, and carefully weighs specially milled hard white flour when making the bread dough.

A third brother-in-law (who just happens to be a master of baking challah bread) has determined that he will set his own pace when renovating his daughter and son-in-law's house. Not wanting to be rushed and not wanting to do shoddy work, he has set his standards and is sticking to them — as a retiree has the power, privilege, and right to do.

Small enjoyments

For in the dew of little things the heart finds its morning and is refreshed.
– Khalil Gibran

Consider the small things that make a life good: chocolate melting in your mouth, the smell of wood smoke, the sound of rain on the windows, the crinkle around a friend's eyes when they laugh, and the glitter of sunlight on water droplets.

Recently, I've had the pleasure of relishing the perfect cherry pie, challah, and oatmeal chocolate chip cookies that my brothers-in-law make in abundance.

Small needs

When you are older you will understand how precious little things, seemingly of no value in themselves, can be loved and prized above all price when they convey the love and thoughtfulness of a good heart. – Edwin Booth

Saying no to the seduction of material things is a relief. I notice, as people age, they want to give belongings away, to stop buying and collecting, to downsize, and to simplify. I know I have started thinking this way. Maybe it's because I helped clear out stuff after my mother, and then my father, died. The stuff they left behind somehow lost its meaning and value when no longer tied to the person, except maybe for a few precious little things. It made me examine my things more critically.

I now choose to watch commercial-free movies in place of television, and no longer receive a newspaper, preferring to receive the news by radio or digitally. This has meant that I do not see advertising or receive many fliers. It's peaceful not being bombarded by images of things that are supposedly essential to my happiness, items I must purchase. I'm enjoying needing less.

In retirement we can seek the simplicity of smaller spaces, small vacations, and a smaller footprint on this planet. We can make time for small acts of kindness, small accomplishments, and small enjoyments. We can look inside to the small person we once were and be content with what we find. That small person was pretty darn perfect. It makes me wonder what we were striving for all these years.

I don't believe this is new in my retirement, but focusing on what has meaning to me seems to happen more easily when my plate is less crowded with others' needs. – Barb

Leaving behind a life legacy that goes beyond ego

By Mariella Hoy

Overview

What is a life legacy — beyond ego — and does it matter if we are intentional about the kind of legacy we want to leave?

On March 1, 2009, after attending his brother-in-law's funeral and hearing of the many public services in which he had been involved, my 88-year-old father wistfully said, "I wonder what they'll say about me." He wondered if he had done enough in his life, if his eulogy would be so glowing. Four years later, August 28, 2013, at the age of 92, he died. Was his eulogy glowing? It was, not so much for public service — although he had done more than most — but for the small, wonderful things he did for those dear to him. More on that in a minute...

Legacy beyond ego

When I mention the idea of leaving a life legacy, the response I often get is cringing. My family and friends don't like the traditional definition of life legacy — being remembered as someone who did something great. That is not to say that they don't want to be remembered by those they love after they've died — they do! But they don't accept the idea that we need a building or street named after us, or reverence paid to us.

Life legacy can be defined as the way you've changed the way people think and act, long after you've been forgotten.

One of my sisters summed it up nicely in a question: "How will the world be different because I was in it?" Think of it as the ripple effect you have.

My brother suggested that we can live a life that leaves a good legacy simply by living well... without focusing on the goal of leaving a good legacy... leaving ego out of it. And my brother-in-law believes that we strive to live an exemplary life if we have that tendency, not because we want to leave a better legacy.

So, whether we strive to or not, how do we change the way people think and act because of the way we live our lives? How can we leave a ripple effect that goes beyond ego?

Bernard's legacy

Back to my father. Bernard hand-wrote a 32-page autobiography detailing his family upbringing, wanderlust, high school shenanigans, meeting and marrying my mother, work experiences and moves to different cities, family life, his faith, retirement, house renovations, travel, and his second marriage. These are the conditions that make a life. Although interesting, the autobiography doesn't tell the true worth of the man. It is more about doing, than being.

What came out at his funeral service were the small ripple effects that mean so much to those he shared his life with — his 10 children. Random snippets of Dad's life were read from a letter written 16 years prior to his death. The letter was called the piggyback letter and was written by my three brothers, six sisters and me. It was a letter of memories and reflections of our lives together. We called it the piggyback letter because one person started it off and then sent it by snail mail to the next sibling, who added their memories and any corrections or notes to the previous person's recollections. We gave the final letter to Mum and Dad for their 50th anniversary (July 31, 1999).

Here are a few of the small memories from that letter, memories of Bernard's rich legacy:

- Dad built us a toboggan slide out of snow in the front yard, sealing it with freezing water.
- Dad said that, whatever the finances, he and our mother wanted to take care of teeth and feet; so new shoes that fit for everyone and milk at every meal.
- He didn't judge people by their appearance. It was part of his great strength of seeing all people as people.
- He had a unique list of expressions of dubious origin:
  - You'd have to hunt around, peck around, snort around to find any luckier rib-rab-rhubarb rabbits
  - Ho-dly-ding-dang, ding-dang, ding-dang!
  - Uppty-duppty — rise and shine. Time for uplin' and dupplin'!
- He was steady and unflappable.
- Dad made exotic cakes — multi-layered with bright shocking pink filling oozing out.
- Dad would read to a row of kids on the couch — him in the middle.
- We came home from a holiday when Dad had to stay behind and he'd painted the entire kitchen, cupboards and all, white! Beautiful — a treat for Mum.

- The wonderfully engineered eight-man bunk bed / dining table with benches ingeniously fitted into the trailer.
- I loved seeing Mum and Dad laugh while having a pillow fight together.

Greatness in small acts

Legacy is a sliver of light in a dark place. It is a lesson on how to love, or how to play. A scent that stirs a fond memory. The comfort of good food. A feeling that justice has been served. A sense of safety and belonging.

Seemingly small acts have great impact. Martin Luther King Jr said, "Not all of us can be famous, but all can be great." Small acts can create great change in other people's ways of being. Generations carry the effect. And, as my sister points out, let's not forget that much of who we are is a direct legacy of the generations before us, from our relationships with them, but also less directly through the impact of books and education.

On the wings of hope

I look at the lives of my friends, clients, and family members and delight in the ripple effects they are creating:

- Discovering ways of managing personal fear and suffering
- Listening to friends, appreciating them, and loving them, with the understanding that love is pivotal to making the world a better place
- Planting a vegetable patch and tending it with children... then those children doing the same with their children
- Working to understand men who have been violent toward women
- Helping the walking wounded, as one of the walking wounded
- Creating beauty and pleasure in a garden, a cake, or a bar of soap
- Proliferating ways of questioning and thinking, through social justice teachings on race, gender, sexual orientation, and class
- Modelling confidence during crisis, as a midwife's mentor
- Transforming ugly houses into places of beauty and comfort

Legacy, ready or not...

We build our legacy every day, in every relationship, and in every human interaction. We shape our legacy when we're cranky, tired, depressed, or sick, just as we do when we're elated, on top of the world, and operating at our best.

I've asked myself if it matters if we are intentional about the ripples we create. My conclusion is yes, it matters. What we do and how we live will impact the world. Like the wings of a butterfly, however small our movements, we do impact the winds, and those winds can sweep across faraway lands. The more we are intentional about living well, the likelier that we'll have a warm and beneficial influence.

It's in the being

My father wondered if he had done enough with his life. I suspect he thought a glowing eulogy meant an impressive list of services to the community, mountains climbed, and summits reached. The 'doing' in life. For me, the 'being' matters more. If we were suddenly rendered unable to do, how would we choose to be? Most of us, fortunately, are fully functioning and can both do and be. It is up to us to decide how we want the world to be different because we were in it. I think how we choose to be will have a bigger impact than what we choose to do.

Dad left three generations of people who prize education and fitness. Three generations who pay attention to a good pair of shoes, dental health, and pineapple upside-down cake. But he also left a multitude of people who are kind and playful, who put boxer shorts on their heads at birthday parties, and eat three desserts at a go. Who whistle while they work. And people who, when seized by a rush of goodwill, will shout ho-dly-ding-dang, din g-dang, ding-dang.

❓ Self-Coaching Questions

The most profound sense of happiness is experienced through the meaningful life, achieved if one exercises one's unique strengths and virtues in a purpose greater than one's own immediate goals. – Martin Seligman

Finding Meaning and Well-Being in Retirement

If Annie Dillard is correct in saying "How we spend our days is how we spend our lives," how would you like to spend your days?

In your search for meaning, what might be some fun things to experiment with?

If you were to spend a slightly larger portion of time simply being, rather than busily doing, what might improve in your life?

In seeking simplicity, what small acts of kindness, small accomplishments, and small enjoyments would you enjoy incorporating into your week?

In what way — big or small — would you like the world to be different because you once lived?

As my sister asked, "When we remember people in our lives, how did they touch us, in memorable ways?" What can we learn from them, to enhance our own lives?

Following Frank into retirement: Retirement — made it!

A very long weekend

In retrospect, I guess it may not have been the best decision to stop work just before the holidays. I arrived home from my last day of work to celebrate with Suzanne and two of our three kids and their partners. They in turn had just finished their exams and were visiting us on their vacation break. Everyone was pretty much in a party mood befitting the time of year and so I easily morphed into vacation mode — eating, drinking, relaxing, eating, visiting, wishing for snow... It is now eight days into my retirement and the penny has yet to drop that I'm not returning to work in the new year.

Feeling naked

My last week of work was jam-packed with meetings, lunches, and dinners, as I continued the transfer of my responsibilities to John, the "new guy." Each meeting brought me a little thrill knowing that I would not have to follow up on any of the action items identified. On Wednesday evening, I filed my last expense reports, cleaned up my hard drive and left appropriate departing messages on my Blackberry, office phone and Outlook. Thursday morning, I loaded all work-related electronics in a box and gave them to John to return to our head office. It was in my car on the six-hour drive home that the weirdness started happening.

Usually on a long drive, I take the opportunity to make numerous calls and my head buzzes with work plans and tasks needing to be done. This time there was no work to think about and, while I enjoyed the sunny break in the weather and the beautiful scenery travelling down Highway 69, I felt distinctly uncomfortable that I no longer had my phone to call a friend or two, to annoy them with my good mood. My dismay deepened on thinking that on my return home I wouldn't have to return calls, check e-mails, or do any last-minute requests. Despite feeling ebullient about leaving work behind, I was feeling a bit like a turtle out of its shell. I no longer had my cloak of status, my shield of twice-monthly paycheques, and my trusty electronics that served me so well in battling never-ending tasks. I was alone with myself and was feeling uneasy staring myself in the eyes. Good thing there were lots of people at home waiting for me!

Mañana

The first thing to go was my awareness of the days of the week. I have no idea which day is which after only eight days. On any long vacation I would count down the days until I had to go back to work, jealously hoarding my time. Now I don't care. Anything that needed to be done soon, no longer needs to be. Tasks that I had postponed until my retirement have been indefinitely shelved until I feel like it. The days are short and the wood fire is warm.

Although I am starting to feel the first inklings of internal pressure to establish a new routine, I figure it will be about two to three months before I finally burst out of my cocoon and test my wings. In the meantime, Suzanne and I have booked up the rest of December and all of January with visits and trips, because we want to and we can! By the time February rolls around, I'll probably be itching to start romping in the snow and working around our house. And if not, then I'll give it another month or two or three.

The world is my oyster and I'm in no particular hurry.

Retirement can be a game changer for relationships at home, particularly between spouses. Retirement changes the circumstances of that relationship. The 40- to 60-hour work week is now gone and it takes some time for partners to adjust to that. Which person likes to be more active? Who wants to be more social — see friends, go to concerts, host parties, and talk to strangers when travelling? And how will the household chores be reallocated? It's like being newlyweds again. Everything needs to be reconsidered, renegotiated.

In this chapter, we'll hear from a number of retired people who describe what it's like to be suddenly living together, full-time, in retirement — the irritants, the surprises, and what makes it worthwhile. You'll find a list of what's important in a relationship, as well as some ideas to help things along. I describe the year my spouse took a sabbatical from teaching — a practise retirement — and how his incursion into my home office was like Goldilocks invading the home of the Three Bears. You'll hear how retirement is like a home decorating project. Finally, you'll find the results of a survey question I distributed to my newsletter subscribers. The question was this: If you have a partner, how did retirement affect your relationship, both for better and for worse?

Articles in this chapter:

- *What makes (or breaks) relationships in retirement*
- *Underfoot*
- *When one person retires and their partner does not*
- *Retirement: The 3Rs — Renew, Refresh, Rejuvenate*
- *Survey responses — How did retirement affect your relationship with your partner?*
- *Self-coaching questions*

What makes (or breaks) relationships in retirement?

By Mariella Hoy

Overview

In this article, I outline what I think is important in relationships. As well, I've listed ideas for keeping relationships vital.

A young friend of mine was asking me the other day about what keeps couples together over the long haul. What makes for a good relationship, one that lasts many years? What breaks a long-term love relationship? This young friend is in her mid-twenties, that phase of life when one chooses a long-term partner. It occurred to me that many couples entering retirement are revisiting these same questions.

When we retire from our busy work lives, suddenly we are thrown together from morning to night and from night to morning, day after day. Absolute bliss — for some — for a while. It would certainly be absolute bliss for a hormone-driven couple of teenagers, drunk on love, hopped up on lust, and absolutely new to the experience of a relationship. In retirement, however, we're both used to and unused to this state of being together as much as we want to be.

If we've come to rely on the constant interactions that we have with people at work all day, what do we do when we're sharing the day with only one other person? Will we show them our favourite talking dog video clip, tell anecdotes, read aloud snippets from a book, tell them our thoughts, and probe for reactions? Will we quietly delve into a long-awaited project, work on solving a problem that we never had time to concentrate on before, or settle into a satisfying read.

What happens when one day, unexpectedly, one of us is feeling unseen and uncared for, and the other is feeling irritated by interruptions and guilty about asking to be left alone. What happened to the lovely balance and harmony that existed before, when we were both working?

What to look for in a partner — my list

Back to my young friend and her question about what keeps couples together over the long haul. I told her that I'm no expert on relationships, having had only one long-term love — albeit for over four decades — but, in spite of my lack of partners, I had made note of what worked over the years, in my relationship and in the long-term relationships around me. I told her that I used to spiel off this list of What to Look for in a Partner to my kids every now and again in the hope that they were listening. Here's my list:

1. **Values** – Pick a partner who has similar values as you, so that your views are aligned on the bigger issues — how to discipline children, what kind of society you want to live in, what money represents for you, what kind of lifestyle you need, how to treat those who differ from you, etc.

2. **Humour** – Find someone who makes you laugh, someone who tickles your funny bone. And one who laughs with you, with gusto!

3. **Belief in you** – Choose someone who believes in you and your potential, someone who will encourage and support you. We're very good at putting ourselves down, so it is important that the person we live with sees our best, even when we don't.

4. **Family relationships** – It helps a lot if the partner you pick has seen good relationships modelled by parents or close family members. Have they learned to love well and to receive love well?

5. **Family genes** – I was once told that you should check out the genes of your prospective partner's family, to see what kind of illnesses run in the family. I consider this optional, at best!

6. **Wallpapering skills** – Of course, before settling on a partner, first try wallpapering a room in an old house together (my mother's advice).

Additions to the list

I was talking to some friends recently and they added a few gems to the list. Here's what they said is important in a relationship:

- Not trying to change the other
- Interest in the others' interests
- Good sex and the memory of good sex
- Money (to relieve the stress some situations produce)
- Having a lively life (even if it's just lively conversation while watching TV together)
- Having independent friendships and interests (like a passion for preserving local buildings)
- Kindness

I find it affirming to discover that many of the attributes on my list (and my friends' lists) appear on the list put together by Karl Pillemer, a gerontologist at Cornell University. In his book *30 Lessons for Living: Tried and True Advice from the Wisest Americans,* he outlines the life lessons learned by more than 1000 adults, 65 years of age or older. These life lessons relate to love, marriage, work and parenting.

If you don't have a partner, and don't want one, how would you like to stay connected when work is no more? If you're looking for a partner, or evaluating whether to stay in your current relationship, it won't hurt to review the lists above, and check out Pillemer's book.

Retirement can be a game changer

Retirement can be a game changer for relationships, causing a shift in how partners view their place in the relationship. The 40-hour work week is now a 40-hour home week. Who gets the couch by the window? Who is more extroverted, more in need of outdoor fitness, happier reading late into the night? Which one communicates by talking it through, which one presents a fully-formed conclusion? Is lunch a time to eat together? Who will take charge of bill payment, lawncare, and grocery shopping? Is love deep enough to hold the couple together?

Here are some ideas for keeping a relationship vibrant:

1. **The 4-Hour Rule**
   Now, some people fear that retirement will mean sitting on the couch together all day, looking out the window, waiting for someone to call, all conversation dried up. In one of my retirement workshops, a participant gave us "The 4-Hour Rule." She said that couples should spend at least four hours apart each day, so that when the two of them come together again they can have a rich, animated conversation.

2. **Focus on what you love about them**
   What do you do if your partner is driving you crazy? I think it helps to look for the things you love about them. Focus on those. What would you miss if your partner were gone? Imagine how completely endearing they were as a young child and how that is still very much a part of them (on some days more than others!) This approach doesn't mean being blind to the things that drive you crazy, but remind yourself of the "Don't Try to Change Them" rule.

3. **Relationships are not static**

And let's not forget that relationships are not static, whether they're a mere 4 days old or if they've lasted 44 years. We continually learn things about ourselves and our partner, we develop new interests and ways of doing things, and, just like everything in nature, we change — gradually, inexorably. It took me 40 years to understand that my partner Mark is extremely literal. It took me almost that long to realize the extent to which my learning style is visual, how little auditory information sticks. His hearing has changed; he no longer hears the high notes, certain bird calls. My skin has become sensitive to certain types of clothing. These are all little things, but it's the little things that matter. I find that if I adopt the notion that my relationship is constantly changing, it prompts me to check in with my partner more often, to see how he is doing, to see how we are doing.

Wrapped in duvets and birdsong

I wonder what will happen when Mark and I are both retired. Will that lovely balance and harmony that currently exists be put to the test? I'm sure it will.

However, I can't think of anything better than spending my days with Mark, whether retired or not. Spontaneously dashing off to see a movie, and sneaking a stash of chocolate into the theatre like bad children. Or sitting outside in the cool spring air, wrapped in duvets, pointing out the different bird calls to each other. Or propped up in bed at night, reading *Pride and Prejudice* aloud. Or taking an early morning drive (in the pre-pandemic days) along roads we've never travelled, in search of morning-mist photos and a greasy-spoon breakfast spot.

When retirement threatens our equanimity, we'll have to find ways to rebalance. Meanwhile, we're hanging on tightly, making "sport for our neighbours", and enjoying each other — wrinkles, warts, foibles, and all.

Underfoot

By Helen
Retired University Professor of English and Women's Studies

Overview

Helen tells of the dance between partners in retirement when sharing a space. The steps in the dance involve knowing when to communicate, when not to interrupt, when to play the flugelhorn, and when to keep that moose-in-a-swimming pool video to yourself.

I have a friend who kept working because her husband retired, and she would find it difficult to be at home full time with him constantly underfoot. I had no such worries about my own retirement, since my partner Thomas and I had spent stretches of workdays together — as academics we sometimes worked at home — and research summers and sabbaticals as well. Besides, our offices were at opposite ends of the house.

What I had feared was that, without the stimulus of the workplace, we would be deprived of independent input and would lack new things to talk about. But as Thomas said recently about that danger, "we can only hope." Apparently, what has happened is that I have become a babbler. My friends and art group and pagan group and women's group and community events and books provide me with a great deal to recount. And Thomas is so often immersed in writing, reading, or practising music, that he either doesn't hear me or doesn't appreciate being interrupted.

Not long ago, Thomas reported that I had just disrupted his television watching fourteen times. On the Internet, particularly Facebook and emails, I find much of interest, not just photos of moose in swimming pools, however endearing, but also accounts of outrageous laws passed in Texas or tips by fellow writers or news of corporate wrongdoing. Some I feel compelled to share. When a friend complained at Women's Week of her husband's interruptions, I reported Thomas's complaint, and shortly thereafter she described her husband as "doing a Helen."

If I ask Thomas whether I talk too much or aimlessly, he refuses to answer, comparing the question to that loaded query about whether one's butt is too fat. But something has changed, and that, for me, may be the biggest surprise yet about retirement. If someone was going to be underfoot, I didn't expect it to be me.

By the same token, Thomas has taken up horn playing, first a borrowed trumpet, then two flugelhorns and a cornet. He practises devotedly. Friends hear blatting in the background to our phone conversations. *Smile, though Your Heart Is Breaking* accompanies me to bed at night. As I said to him, "I have come to appreciate the harmonica."

Both of us used to be kept busier and quieter by our work.

— **"** ————————————————————————

If someone was going to be underfoot, I didn't expect it to be me. – Helen

———————————————————————— **"** —

When one person retires and their partner does not

By Mariella Hoy

Overview

A number of years ago, my partner took a year's leave from teaching. At that time, I wrote about what I learned from that year, a year in which he practised retirement and I tried to keep working in my home-office.

If my partner Mark weren't practising retirement this year, I wouldn't have had the chance to help move an 800-pound rock this morning before work.

Mark, an elementary school science teacher, is taking a year-long sabbatical from teaching. To establish routine for his 60-week 'lolliday,' he created a schedule for his mornings, for projects like canoe repairs, tree trimming, fence rebuilding, and bathroom renovations. The first time slot each day is for gardening.

That's what he was doing when he discovered the 800-pound rock. It was buried in a garden he was reclaiming. Rather than rebury it, he decided to remove it. "It's the challenge of it more than anything," he said. He went on to say, "Archimedes said, 'Give me a lever long enough and a fulcrum on which to place it, and I shall move the world.'" So, we moved the world — 17 inches west — and I learned about levers, fulcrums and come-along winches. Moving that rock for no good reason was as useful as many advertising campaigns, political skirmishes, and personal squabbles we see in the world around us.

Life shifts 17 inches west when one person retires and their partner does not. This I've learned so far in Mark's practise year.

Variety, spontaneity, languor, and love

I work from a home office. Since the school year ended in June, life has been awash with brilliant colour. Variety, spontaneity, languor, and love came together in a perfect summer storm. We have Happy Hour on nights other than the customary Friday night. Most nights seem to be happy. Days too. Throughout the day, we shout questions back and forth, from my office upstairs to the kitchen or outside where he spends most of his time: Did you get that email from Sylvie? Did you see the pink hollyhock blooming out back? Should we play 'jeez' for 70 points in Word with Friends? Did you notice that the flycatcher babies have flown? How do you spell perseverance?

Changes are happening around our property too. Mark is rebuilding our 30-year-old cedar rail fences. He has created new paths through the woods, limbed dozens of cedar trees to let the sunset stream through, and moved our winter supply of firewood into the woodshed, refusing my help. This is the first time in 23 years I have not moved firewood. And I have never seen Mark's vegetable patch so weed-free either.

Goldilocks has entered my den

I recognize the honeymoon rose-tinted glasses even as I peer through them. They haven't blinded me to the less appealing aspects of this practise retirement... a block of cheese on the counter after the breakfast clear-up; dirty socks and dishes in the living room overnight; boots in the middle of the kitchen Monday to Friday, instead of just weekends; the radio volume turned higher than comfortable for my ears; the front door left wide open; the cacophony of the chainsaw outside my office window. Every day, the chair I usually sit in for lunch is taken. Goldilocks has entered my den.

Setting crankiness aside

I find myself prematurely facing the adjustments many couples struggle with when one retires and the other does not. I could let myself get edgy about these less-pleasing changes, but it doesn't take long before I remember the wonderful developments I've seen in Mark since he went on vacation. Amazingly, he often gets a full night of sleep now, instead of the five or six hours of broken sleep he gets during the school year. I can't remember when this last happened, if ever. And I often find him sitting restfully — reading, contemplating — instead of his usual two speeds: full-tilt or asleep. He is now writing — a lifelong desire. He's chuckling his way through a musical he is writing for school children, a science/nature play about saving the school property from evil gravel-pit developers. And he's writing cocky emails to our kids. "I am struggling through yet another week off — I'm getting a bit edgy, though, because I only have 60 weeks left before school starts again." Smug clown!

Lessons learned

Like Mark, I have a year to practise for his full retirement. What have I learned so far?

- When couples are involved, retirement isn't an individual decision.
- Time off work to practise retirement is a damn good idea. Wouldn't it be wonderful if more organizations offered a sabbatical plan like our teachers get? For example, one model is a three-over-four plan, in which 25% of a teacher's

pay is deferred over three years, and then the teacher is paid 75% salary during the fourth year, the leave-of-absence year. Unfortunately, few people get this option, and most people can't take a whole year off without ruining their pension, depleting their savings, or both. However, it might be well worth it for those of us still working to take small blocks of vacation, to try out something we think we'd like to do in retirement.

- I'm better off during this practise year directing my attention toward the good things, rather than focussing on small irritants that arise because Mark is in my quiet, controlled workspace.

- I'm going to have to consider my own place in Mark's retirement, when he chooses to leave work permanently. I always assumed I'd carry on doing what I'm doing, because I'm having fun, but now I think I'll keep my mind open to other possibilities — even extraordinary ones.

Mark is cherishing the limited amount of time he has off work, an approach he finds much more manageable than when contemplating the expanse of full retirement. Like moving an 800-pound rock, I guess it helps to look at retirement as incremental shifts over time, instead of as a daunting prospect. Whether adjusting to Mark's retirement or settling into my own, I take heart knowing that, with a little help, I can shift myself, and the world, one delightful inch at a time.

Retirement: The 3 Rs — Renew, Refresh, Rejuvenate

Donna Beatty
Retired Community Health Promotion Consultant

> ## Overview
>
> *Retirement renews, refreshes, and rejuvenates us, our home, our friendships, and our relationship with our life partner. All it takes is a little time, a lot of thought, and some flexibility to get the job done.*

I love retirement! I am very grateful for the presence of a loving partner and family, good health, and a monthly pension. All these factors have contributed in a large way to a happy retirement. However, it has taken time and much thought, both before and after retirement, to reach this state of contentment.

Relationships

I've been surprised by changing friendships after retirement. As the time away from an active work life increases, my contact with former work buddies is drastically reduced. Now, friends and social life revolve around shared interests and activities. Childhood friends that I had lost contact with have reappeared and several loyal, long-time friends are always nearby. Friendship becomes a nice mixture of the old and new.

In retirement, I've developed closer ties with my grandchildren. What a treat this has been. I have to say, though, helping out with the grandkids can take a lot of time. I find I have to be quite flexible with my planning.

Every retired person will tell you that their relationship with their significant other is different after retirement. My partner and I retired at different times. A wonderful advantage of a couple retiring at different times is that the first to retire has, hopefully, established a new routine. Better yet is when that new routine includes the household tasks which the still-to-retire partner has mastered and wants to pass on... for example, cooking and grocery shopping. I am fortunate to have a dear partner who not only cooks but looks on food shopping as an adventure. I cook some meals and help with the meal planning. I am quite okay with giving up the title of Chief Cook — what's not to like about this arrangement?

Remember the title of that old movie: *The Good, the Bad, and the Ugly?* Long-term relationships can be a lot like that. The positive news is that, once again, we have time for each other, our shared interests, and our family. With lots of love and humour, we're learning to accept (and/or tolerate) both the similarities and the differences in our individual interests.

Other Changes

There is one other area that has changed because of retirement — our home — both inside and out. Now that I have more time and am spending it at home, I see things from a different perspective.

I've been surprised, too, that I actually worry less about money now than when I was working. I'm not sure why, but we're managing on less coming in, and doing much better than I expected.

Retirement is like home decorating

I find similarities between the notions of home decorating projects and retirement. The same principles apply: renew, refresh, and rejuvenate. In retirement, just as we need to freshen things up with our house, so too with ourselves. We may choose to get rid of some things, rearrange others, and occasionally introduce something new. The result: we become renewed, refreshed, and rejuvenated. Although it has taken time and a good deal of thought, I think I'm there.

Okay, I may not be hot, but I'm still passionate. So don't dismiss me just yet. – Anson

Survey Responses: How did retirement affect your relationship with your partner?

By Mariella Hoy

Overview

In an issue of the Retiring with Purpose and Passion newsletter, the following question was asked: "If you have a partner, how did retirement affect your relationship, both for better and for worse?"

Responses showed a rich diversity of answers, as varied as people themselves, as interesting as couples can be. Some couples became closer in retirement, working through the irritants of suddenly sharing more time together. Others carried on the same as before, without noticing any significant differences. A couple of people told us that they now face retirement alone, having lost their partners to illness — a sobering thought, indeed.

Responses to the question "If you have a partner, how did retirement affect your relationship, both for better and for worse?"

1. My challenge was learning how to accept my life of retiring without my spouse. Sadly, he got ill as I retired and I spent the first part of my retirement caregiving. Now I am alone and retired and learning how to rebuild my retirement plans as a single person.

2. Because we both had flexibility in our work hours and worked a fair bit at home together over the years, I didn't anticipate being an intrusion in my partner's space when I retired. But being less pressured by work (and earlier child-care responsibilities), I had more time and freedom to engage with him then, for better but also for worse. We had to find new ways to have separate spaces, both being introverts.

3. We get to see an awful lot of each other. Make time for togetherness and for separate activities.

4. Much doesn't change, it just becomes clearer that we are still the same people. The better side — we've developed positive patterns over the years which can be nurtured. The worse — health does change, and we don't necessarily have the same skills to live with those changes as the ones we're used to.

5. We go for walks 4+ days per week providing a great time to talk about short- and long-range plans and how we are feeling. I'm also reaching out to friends to do activities — walks, lunches, plays, outings.

6. Less stress

7. Some people would drive each other crazy being together 24/7, but we are lucky to enjoy each other's company.

8. For the better, as we can now both pursue the things we want to as a couple and as individuals.

9. Relationship no better or worse than before. We have more freedom to travel together, which is nice, especially spending time in the south during the winter. At home, we keep separate schedules during the week, just as we did when we were working, and that seems to work well for us.

10. I lost my husband very early on. We did have one great vacation after I retired and before he got sick and it was wonderful. We were on the same page as far as travelling and our interest in other countries and cultures.

11. We've had some health challenges that have brought us closer together.

12. I don't see that my relationship with my spouse has changed. Certainly, there have been minor irritations with each other, but these have been worked through like we have done in the past decades of marriage.

13. My husband hasn't retired yet. So, we're not in each other's way. I reflect a more relaxed and positive mien, because of my peace of mind. This, therefore, also reflects on our relationship.

14. My husband, who is still working, is appreciating that I am no longer working. I make myself available to do things that ordinarily he would have had to do. I enjoy preparing our evening meal and that is certainly appreciated as well.

15. Our 'togetherness' all day long, every day often proved too much for me. I was in fact invading his space since his previous work was done from home. I learned to go out for lunch once every two weeks and walk 5 days out of 7. I like my independence and didn't want to drop into the role of cook, laundress, and housekeeper, just because I was now home more.

16. We have individual interests, which we happily pursue with support from one another; at the same time, we do spend a lot of time together without rubbing each other the wrong way.

17. Relationship much better.

18. My partner and I have a greater acceptance of each other's individuality and that is a good thing.

? Self-Coaching Questions

For retirement brings repose, and repose allows a kindly judgment of all things. – John Sharp Williams

Adjusting Relationships at Home

Given that the 8-hour workday will now be spent at home together, how much of a separate bubble do you need from your spouse each day? By that I mean:

- time apart doing separate activities
- headphones to keep music, radio programs, videos, and movies from bothering the other
- space to yourself, like an office, coffee shop, den, sitting area, or workshop
- separate friendship time
- independent means of transportation
- space to work around each other in the kitchen, etc.

What do you love about your partner?

What conversation might be useful for smoothing foreseeable bumps in the road?

What activities would you like to do together — to enjoy each other, to tighten the bond, to celebrate this new phase of life?

Which household roles do you want to be responsible for and which do you not?

Following Frank into Retirement:
1 month into it

The storm before the calm

I've been retired now for almost 1½ months and I'm still trying to get the time to retire. Suzanne and I have slept in 10 different beds during that time, and have spent a total of 5 days at home in the month of January. I was eager (and somewhat trepidatious) to return home from our travels so that I could experience life at home as a retiree. Unfortunately, I've been back for three days now and life just keeps getting in the way of my plans. Plumbing problems, stained carpet, and pension transfer forms have sucked away my time and energy. I'm feeling very impatient with my lack of progress towards discovering my true passion (besides Suzanne). I haven't even had the chance to get my bagpipes ready to play.

Forms and more forms

Before rambling madly off in all directions, I would first like to vent my spleen about financial companies and their forms. I am delighted that I have some pension from my last 9½ years of employment. However, my joy has been tempered by the half day that Suzanne and I spent filling out ambiguous forms, digging up the required information, and calling representatives for clarification. I don't like forms at the best of times, but the lack of adequate instructions and vague requests for information made this task a real chore. To add insult to injury, the only number listed in one company's letter was to their sales department, giving them one more chance to hang on to our funds. Suzanne and I are both well educated and experienced professionals. How do people without training manage? It seems that these companies are purposely being obstructionist by trying to prevent retirees from transferring funds away from them.

Whew! That felt almost as good as mailing off those forms.

Taking leave

Another task I did was clean out my work desk. I took several boxes of files to the dump to be recycled and boxed up my reference texts that still seem to function as my security blanket. While the purged work area was definitely a step forward, it was an uncomfortable experience to dismantle my work of the past 30+ years. While not in the least nostalgic for my work, I recognized that I was bringing to a close an aspect of my life to which I had devoted considerable time and energy; an area in which I had expertise, confidence and respect. I do not expect to return to my profession. It was a bit of a downer, which fortunately disappeared with the tossing of the last box into the recycling bin.

Patience is a virtue

In this age of instant gratification, learning to wait patiently for your life to unfold could be difficult. I feel like a little kid that desperately wants to be bigger. I can't wait to grow up. Every day not spent exploring possibilities seems like a wasted day; another day in limbo. My work has trained me to set and achieve goals with the constant reward of a paycheque. I have to figure out not only some completely different goals but also a good alternative to my paycheques. I have some good role models — people whose passion for what they do fills their days (and sometimes nights). It worries me that I'll end up just filling in time for the next 30 years. This brings me full circle back to the bit about being patient.

A snake in the grass

As Suzanne and I were driving down to Toronto to meet up with some friends, a new thought slithered its way into my head. I am still relatively young, healthy, and am well respected in my field. Why am I not working? It wasn't a question about working to earn more money; it was a question about why I'm not working when I am still able. It was a strong feeling and it surprised me. Since the thought was emotional, I had no good comeback to allow me to file it in my mind's wastebasket. It made me even more impatient to reboot.

Back to Life

Despite all my concerns, it has been great not working. There has not been a single day pass when I've regretted leaving my work behind. It makes me smile all over just thinking about it. In the meantime, it will have to be one step at a time, maybe even baby steps, as I work my way into retirement. I've got plans, just not big ones. I'm making mushu pork for supper. It's been snowing a lot lately and I'm saving snowblowing my driveway for tomorrow when I can enjoy doing it to the maximum.

Like I said, baby steps.

9 Struggling with the Creative Urge

I've been wondering about creativity — why so many people seek it out in retirement, and why others don't; what lures us to creativity, and what stops us cold; and what conditions support the creative process. In this chapter, I explore these thoughts in *What lures us to creativity?*

Also contained in this chapter is an elementary teacher's trepidation about creativity in his upcoming "practise retirement" sabbatical year, his fear that his perception of himself as a creative person will be tested and may be found to be inaccurate. He gives us his thoughts in two parts:

- Practising retirement, and my cover story (Part 1) - 6 months prior to the sabbatical
- Practising retirement, and my cover story (Part 2) - at the end of the 14-month sabbatical

Then, in 'Getting back to the dreams,' you can read about a retiree who became a therapist as part of his retirement, but struggles with a "need to express things, to conceive, to produce, to capture beauty and put it into some form, to touch emotions and express them." He worries that his work as a therapist is taking precedence over his need to create.

The final article in the chapter — What it all means — a retired professor probes whether or not her strong work ethic is overpowering playfulness in the process of painting.

Articles in this chapter:

- *What lures us to creativity?*
- *Practising retirement, and my cover story (Part 1)*
- *Practising retirement, and my cover story (Part 2)*
- *Getting back to the dreams*
- *What it all means*
- *Self-coaching questions*

What lures us to creativity?

By Mariella

Overview

Creativity helps us experience our world deeply, giving us appreciation for what's around us, even adding to our understanding of ourselves. This article broadens the definition of creativity, lists its benefits, discusses the fear we feel when wanting to become creative, and touches on some of the conditions that foster creativity.

The notion of creativity has got me wondering. What draws us to be creative? And why are the blank page and blank canvas so intimidating? What do we need to have in place to support our creative process? In looking for answers, I dug out an old file in which I had gathered a collection of my favourite ideas from books I was reading at the time, books on the subjects of creative writing, philosophy, and life. I was doing some writing then and was finding the creative process to be both alluring and scary. That was 20 years ago. I've made some small headway in my thinking, with the help of many authors, philosophers and thinkers who have expressed their thoughts so well. I'd like to share some of those insights here.

In *Care of the Soul,* Thomas Moore suggests that art gives us a way to engage deeply in our lives, preventing the emptiness that comes when we aren't paying attention. He said, "Naturally, we'll feel empty if everything we do slides past without sticking. As we have seen, art arrests attention, an important service to the soul. Soul cannot thrive in a fast-paced life because being affected, taking things in and chewing on them, requires time."

The creative process deepens our experience of living. We need time to chew over our experiences: to stop, observe, and reflect. All people are meaning-seeking and meaning-making. Creating something gives us that chance to find meaning in what we are experiencing.

Broadening the definition of creativity

Joyce Wycoff describes creativity as making brand new connections between things, connections everyone else has missed. It's a treasure hunt for what has not yet been found. What we create will be unique, because our experiences, backgrounds, and personalities are unique.

Now, some people insist they aren't interested in being creative, or that they don't have the talent. I suspect, though, that this thinking comes from a narrow definition of creativity — creativity in the limited sense of traditional arts (e.g., painting, music, dance), rather than one's own form of problem solving, or expressing ideas. Robert Franken, in his book *Human Motivation,* identifies three reasons why people are motivated to be creative: the need for novel, varied, and complex stimulation; the need to communicate ideas and values; and, the need to solve problems. When we are creative, we bring imagination, original ideas, and an intention to solve something or communicate something.

I've been totally impressed with my partner's creativity since he retired. He certainly dabbles in the artistic forms of creativity, like singing, acting, and writing, but he has recently expanded into some fascinating problem-solving and "novel, varied, and complex" creativity. When he had to move a huge log by himself, he combined the forces of a farm jack, a cant hook, splitting wedges, and a come-along. When his chisel handle broke, he turned a new handle on the wood lathe. Same deal when he needed a new mallet, and strong mortise-and-tenon sawhorses. When he had 53 timbers to store in the garage, he built a frame for a hoist and lifted these 300- to 500-pound timbers onto a hand-crafted trailer, wheeled the trailer into the garage, where he had set up a second hoist to assist him in stacking the timbers. I've watched him dismantle a stone barn foundation and load the stones on 60 pallets, by himself, without lifting them or hurting his back. Levers, fulcrums, tripods, pulleys, and ratchets are his friends. He has continually created new processes and tools, filling his days with happiness.

How are you creative in ways not seen as traditionally creative? When you plan the landscaping? In how you try unusual ingredients in recipes? In how you repurpose objects? In planning a trip? In how you stimulate and, at the same time, not-overstimulate your grandchild? Are you a persistent inventor, like Thomas Edison? Do you visualize, in fine detail, projects in your imagination, like Nikola Tesla? It's good for us to consider these questions so we can appreciate our own creativity, especially when it goes beyond the narrow definition.

Our brains love to create

A study compared the brain activity of six professional jazz pianists when they played by memory versus when they improvised (PLOS ONE, Limb and Braun, 2008). An MRI machine was connected to a special keyboard and the musicians were asked to play a piece of music straight from memory. They were then asked to improvise. The creativity of improvisation showed up in their brains in three ways — inhibition was switched off, self-expression was switched on, and sensory awareness became heightened. The lesson is clear — regardless of the form, being involved in an act of creativity produces stimuli that lead to fulfillment.

Full-blast living

According to Mihaly Csikszentmihalyi, when we are creating, we come about as close to fulfilment as we can. It is our source for meaningful living. He calls it 'full-blast living'.

Is it any wonder so many people long to create?

Yet, I have heard more than one newly retired person express the idea that creating art is not a worthy undertaking. This notion that art is frivolous is one not shared by Albert Einstein, who said, "The intuitive mind is a sacred gift, the rational mind a faithful servant. We have created a society that honors the servant and has forgotten the gift." How often have we heard intuition scorned and the rational mind praised? What if we were to reverse the value placed on the two?

The terror of the blank canvas

The real sticking point is that, even if we lauded intuition and the creative spirit, we would still be faced with the paralysis that can come from the fear of making fools of ourselves. If only the blank canvas weren't so daunting. If only the prospect of building a timber frame structure weren't so scary. If only we could think with the positivity expressed by George Bernard Shaw, when he said, "A man learns to skate by staggering about making a fool of himself. Indeed he progresses in all things by resolutely making a fool of himself."

In *The Hero's Journey,* Joseph Campbell supported Shaw's notion. In his view, artists are not competing and are not trying to be first in the public eye. They are fulfilling themselves, each uniquely.

The conditions necessary to create

The question then becomes: What will support us in tackling our creative endeavours? Michele Jones, a free-spirited and creative coaching friend, once gave me a list of what she considered to be the conditions necessary to increase, nurture and foster creativity:

- Have courage; trust in yourself
- Be in the moment
- Be open to possibilities
- Respond to gifts presented

- Collaborate with others
- Quiet the mind
- Calm the body

I would add to that:

- See failure as learning
- Balance challenges with skills

If we welcome failure as learning, and if we don't overwhelm ourselves by attempting challenges we aren't prepared for, we may experience creativity in a more playful light. And I can't help thinking that retirement offers us a rare opportunity to set the conditions necessary for creativity.

What draws us to creativity, what stops us cold, and what conditions support the process? I think it is clear that creativity deepens our experience of living and fulfills us. Our brains love the creative process, and that process is unique to every individual. Fear of looking like a fool can stop us cold, but it's okay to stumble around looking like a fool while we learn our craft, because it's not about creating masterpieces. Finally, there are approaches we can take to nurture and foster creativity, keeping us open, trusting, and imaginative.

I wish I could stop condemning myself for not making obvious contributions to the world. I wish I could believe that making beauty is a valuable enough offering. – Helen

Practising retirement, and my cover story (Part 1)

By Mark
Elementary School Teacher

> ## Overview
>
> *Preparing for a sabbatical year away from teaching, Mark is a little nervous that the creative creature hiding inside himself for so long will not come out to play.*

I'm pretty lucky — six months from now, I get to try something very few people ever have the opportunity to try. A practice retirement. All the upsides and downsides without the concomitant case of nerves leading up to the big day.

I am a school teacher. Fifteen years ago, at age 45, I left the legal profession and returned to school to qualify as an elementary teacher. I love what I do. Every single day I walk through my school with a smile on my face because I love being around all the people I am around, from Junior Kindergarten to Grade 8 (this year I have classes covering all grade levels from JK to 8!). Nobody should be allowed to have this much fun!

The lure of retirement

I am not, however, a complete Pollyanna. There are always challenges. For me the biggest challenge is being, and feeling, fully prepared to support the learning of my students in a meaningful way. It wears. The last few years I find myself longingly contemplating the situations of the many friends and family members who have retired, and wishing I could just stay home and not have to worry about being adequately prepared for the next day.

So, I count myself lucky that my partner and I decided to bank 25% of my salary for three years so I could take the fourth year off with pay. That year begins in just over six months.

The scarier truth lurking behind my cover story

Many people have asked me what plans I have made for my year off, and my answer is always the same — none. I tell people I do not want to be tied down with plans; that I want to be free to do whatever strikes me in the moment. These things are true, but I think there is a bigger, scarier truth lurking just behind my cover story. There are things that are part of my long-time, ever-since-I-was-a-kid, this-is-at-the-core-of-my-inner-self dreams that I am afraid to butt up against with nowhere else to turn. Because I might fail. We all have them — those deep-seated perceptions we have of our creative selves, whether our creativity is expressed with a pen or a paint brush, a chisel or a cheerful smile, a piano or a *plié*.

I am very active in many ways that have taken me by complete surprise as an adult. When I moved with my family to a secluded 50-acre property near a small Ontario city over 20 years ago, I had never participated in any creative endeavours. Within a few years of arriving here, I had joined an amateur theatre group and a choir. I also began writing — not creative works, but pieces that were able to satisfy, at least initially, that longstanding writing itch. A few years ago, I found myself deeply enthralled with poetry, an infatuation that has led me to a new creative interest in theatre from the dramaturgical perspective.

Focus, dabble, or run for the hills?

Why am I mentioning all this? Because I now have the opportunity to try out a practice 'retirement.' I have many interests to choose from. Have I set myself up for success, or for failure? Can one succeed or fail at retirement? I don't know. I do know that my interests are so many and so varied that I cannot possibly give them all a reasonable try in the course of 14 months. Should I focus on one thing? Should I dabble? Should I avoid the whole question and head to Patagonia?

I'm not really sure. So, for the time being, I am playing it safe and telling people I haven't made any plans; that I'm going to take it easy and see what comes up. Maybe that way, I'll figure out what to expect of myself leading up to my real retirement in a few years. One can only hope.

Practising retirement, and my cover story (Part 2)

By Mark
Elementary School Teacher

Overview

After his sabbatical from teaching, Mark is ready to return to work. Did his creative self come out to play? Mark tells us what having the gift of time at his disposal meant for him and what he learned during his practice retirement year.

Here I am at the end of fourteen months of practice retirement. I think it's fair to say I went into my year off with equal measures of trepidation and confidence. I knew what I wanted to come at, but I wanted to come at those things sideways. Head-on collisions can be cathartic, but they don't always leave us standing.

I wanted my year to be an exploration — a journey through some of the ideas that have bounced around in my head for 61 years (giving myself some credit for being inquisitive as an infant.)

Creative impulses — a flash here and a wiggle there

I love the idea of creating for myself. I just don't feel impelled to undertake a grand work. The garden space I found in a long-neglected load of rocks is a delight I hope many will enjoy, but if none do, it will be there nonetheless. The trees I am trying to form into a forest (arrogant presumption!) are beautiful whether anyone is there to see or not. Our path through the cedars is our place of sanctity and delivers us a moment of joy every time we traverse it.

Photo: Mariella Hoy.

Coming at it sideways

Yet, as I am casting gently into some of those bigger, lying-in-the-weeds ideas, I am allowing myself to come at them sideways, so as not to frighten them back into deeper waters. A flash here and a wiggle there. A theatrical play with music is in the works. I'm getting ready to do some woodworking — bowl-turning especially. I am thinking about rock as art form. I am starting to read some of the books that have been beckoning me for far too long. So, I do have aspirations. I just don't like to fully acknowledge them publicly. Or even to myself.

Those big ever-since-I-was-a-kid, this-is-at-the-core-of-my-inner-self dreams

What have I learned about having the gift of time always at my disposal? Well, I have most certainly learned there are endless opportunities to distract oneself from the things that are important. I notice when I am goofing off, turning aside from that ever-so-casual saunter down the path to where I hope to arrive. Of course, my whole being is defined by the continual expansion of my capacity for goofing off. But not all goofing off is goofing off — one form is purposeful. Examples are the woodworking I enjoy, the time I spend in our various woodlots (always a meditation more than a task), the reading I do, and the retirement businesses I regularly invent (with no particular expectation of launching them — they are more an entertainment for myself and my friends). Other forms of goofing off are not so purposeful, such as the execrable computer word games I play. Such activities are how I am diverted from the path I would rather amble along.

I have in fact butted up against some of those big ever-since-I-was-a-kid, this-is-at-the-core-of-my-inner-self dreams, and the experience was neither as daunting nor as unsuccessful as I expected. I know that I'll be able to continue down that path, apprehensively for certain, but down it nonetheless, when I fully retire.

I have no great expectations of myself when I retire for real — I would like to take a few more steps in the direction I have gone, and see where they lead me. The hard work will be to maintain a modicum of discipline, so I can actually see if I have the ability to achieve what I hope to achieve.

Annoying my sister-in-law

I suppose I have not actually said what my aspirations entail. This will annoy my sister-in-law no end — she who asked for details when I wrote in my first article those many months ago. I told her then, as I am stating now, that I am not prepared to say. Too dangerous — someone may remember.

So where am I today? I have the great gift of actually looking forward to returning to my job of teaching in an elementary school. It is a gift to spend my days with young and very young children who love learning for its own sake. I hope when I finally do retire fully, I will be able to take on some of the challenges I seem to have set myself up for. As long as I can sort of do that without letting anybody know...

— 66 —

I knew what I wanted to come at, but I wanted to come at those things sideways. Head-on collisions can be cathartic, but they don't always leave us standing. – Mark

— 99 —

Getting back to the dreams

By Peter
Retired Primary English Teacher / Curriculum Advisor

Overview

Peter fears that his budding artist is taking a back seat to his post-retirement therapist career. Here he gives us a review of his determined progress and unresolved concerns.

Three years into retirement, after training to become a therapist, I realized that I had a real and urgent need to create. The need wasn't new. It's been there for years. I need to express things, to conceive, to produce, to capture beauty and put it into some form, to touch emotions and express them. I realized that I needed to get back to my dreams.

I have sat in the therapist's chair often, now up to three days a week. But the budding artist is still budding.

Origins of the bud

As a fresh retiree, I moved to a new home and many things changed in my life, including my studies. Instead of nurturing the artist in me, I put that on hold. But I had my dreams ... and a plan which involved getting back to the kid with the recorder and the adult painter with ideas and talent. The plan was to purchase production quality video equipment, microphones, and a portable field mixer and digital recorder. It included renovating the back shed into a studio for the polymorphic artist that I want to be. It also involved going to school to 'upgrade' my technical knowledge of the equipment and accepting help from others who use it.

I came to appreciate that I didn't know how to draw, had stubby fingers and little confidence in myself. I then began to understand that there are entire professions built around the components in my equipment cupboard: camera operator, audio recordist, boom operator, director, producer, lighting supervisor, digital photographer, just to name a few. There also are the artistic factors that go into the creative process of producing the documents that I want to work on. It is not part of my dream to become all that, but I want to be at ease and know what I'm doing.

Update

I concede that the plan has slipped into year 3.5. But I am proud to say the equipment has been purchased, slowly, piece by piece. I enjoyed that, learning about what I should buy, talking to the people that sell it, and taking a few courses. The studio is in place. I enjoyed helping build it and especially designing the work and storage area. The result is an oversized cupboard with shelving, a desk area for drawing, cutting, or working with clay or styrofoam, as well as an enclosed painting surface — all with adequate lighting. The enclosure has doors that shelter my artistic endeavours from the view of therapy clients. I love the office/studio with its large windows looking out on to the lawn and the woods... and the birds.

Wherein lies the rub?

I'm more in the office than the studio, more for my clients and the administration duties linked to my volunteer work. The artist in me is still largely behind closed doors. That, at times, is frustrating. It wouldn't be too bad if I could wait a little. The project time run-over, to get to where I am, wouldn't bother me normally. I have learned to be indulgent towards that part of me where I get sidelined. But there's the rub. I have been putting things on hold for quite a while, yet I'm 66. There's an end to the side track somewhere, and now it's sooner rather than later. That is why I have to stop. Once still, I can determine where I want to go and, more importantly, how I want to get there.

— 66 —

I have in fact butted up against some of those big ever-since-I-was-a-kid, this-is-at-the-core-of-my-inner-self, and the experience was neither as daunting nor as unsuccessful as I expected. – Mark

99 —

What it all means

By Helen
Retired University Professor of English and Women's Studies

> ## Overview
>
> *Helen discusses how the sheer enjoyment of making art for its own sake and the drive to be productive and successful as an artist tug her in two different directions.*

The thing about art is that life is in no danger of being meaningless.
– Robert Genn

I have a busy friend who would treat retirement as time off and who shakes her head at my commitment to painting every weekday. Her partner explains that art is my new job. My Chinese herbalist neighbour urges that, for health, I should be indulging in the opposite of my usual values, should be wandering, being playful, and acting silly. I have to ask myself whether I'm afraid of freedom, needing productivity to feel worthwhile, trapped by that industriousness and work ethic. Am I striving for a new success, as a professional artist, rather than painting for its own sake?

At the same time, I lie awake eagerly creating better paintings in my head than I can get on canvas. Sometimes, when sleeping, I dream of painting. When I travel, images that I'm unable to capture by camera or memory tantalize me. More painfully I'm tormented at times by my inability to realize my vision on canvas.

One of my friends spent this summer dying, and I grieved for her as I worked. When I looked around my studio with joy in my completed paintings stacked against the walls and especially when I imagined more, one of the regrets I felt for her was her loss of just such future possibilities.

The other day I felt sheer pleasure in the colours I was applying — a rich burnt sienna and a phthalo blue-green. No concern then about proving myself or 'being a painter' as opposed to painting. Just enjoyment of the process.

The studio solidifies my commitment to art, moves my retirement more firmly in that direction. And still I work on finding painting's place in my life, as part of a balanced life. In the moment I am given.

？ Self-Coaching Questions

Our deepest fear is not that we are inadequate. Our deepest fear is that we are powerful beyond measure. It is our light, not our darkness, that most frightens us. We ask ourselves, who am I to be brilliant, gorgeous, talented, and fabulous? Actually, who are you not to be?[1] *– Marianne Williamson*

Struggling with the Creative Urge

When were you at your best, when the gifts you were born with and the talents you developed were braided with what you love?

If you consider the three reasons why people are motivated to be creative (the need for novel, varied, and complex stimulation; the need to communicate ideas and values; and, the need to solve problems), how are you creative — maybe in ways not traditionally seen as creative?

When will you make time to simply observe and contemplate?

Which of the conditions necessary for creativity do you need to put in place?

How might you enrich your world through creativity?

---

1 Williamson, M. (1992). *A Return to Love: Reflections on the Principles of a Course in Miracles.* New York: Harpercollins. With permission.

Following Frank into Retirement: 3 months into it

Something's cooking

The strong spring sun is finally overcoming the wintry nights. Early flower shoots, returning birds, and plumping tree buds all are in sync with my emerging life as a retired person (although this year's sporadic flow of maple sap might be a more fitting metaphor). As Suzanne and I gain more experience with our retirement, we find that we are fitting in new activities and tasks to our daily routine that are slowly leading us to a fulfilling retired life. There is a scent in the air of something good cooking (besides my multigrain cheese bread) and my anticipation is growing.

Step by step

In a recent article, I mentioned my progress as a retiree in terms of baby steps. Well, I'm well past baby steps and I'm starting to truck right along. This past month, being retired means that we've been able to apartment hunt in Kincardine for our son and daughter-in-law (while visiting friends and family in Owen Sound). We've also spent three days helping our neighbours to tap their trees in their sugar bush. Another four days disappeared in Ottawa visiting our son, his fiancée and her parents, and some close friends of ours. Fine meals were eaten, wedding dresses hunted, and scotch drunk. Too bad everyone else had to go back to work. We've also been getting out most days for a long walk to our mailbox or in our bush. The cold nights have made it easy to walk on top of the snow in the morning and we've spent a couple of gorgeous days following the remains of the 100-year-old barbed wire fence around our property.

However, our biggest accomplishment so far is that we have started to tile our kitchen backsplash. Now this may not sound like a big step, but when you consider that we have had the tiles stored in our family room for two years (we were just waiting for the right time — honest), this is a big one. It's taken us three days so far and we would have been finished cementing in the tiles today if I didn't have trouble installing a new range hood (the old one was just too gross to be next to our new tile). The flashing and ductwork inside range hoods are razor sharp. Two quick slices and six stitches later,

I'm a wiser and older-feeling renovator. I was most upset about the lost time, but as Suzanne said as she headed out for her afternoon haircut and evening of line-dancing, "No problem, we'll finish it tomorrow". Totally freeing.

There yesterday, gone today

One interesting aspect of my retirement is the complete absence of any thought or interest in my previous career. It is like that portion of my brain has been surgically removed. It just does not even enter into my thoughts except wondering at the changes in me each time we drive by a sawmill or wood products plant. It is slightly worrying that I might have already lost my cutting edge. Furthermore, how much of my quirky and lovable personality was a result of my constant trials and tribulations at work? Will the real Frank the Forester please stand up?

Money in the bank

Money could be my Achilles heel (and all this time I thought it was food). When I wake up at night, it is often money that is on my mind (although our children run a close second). I don't like losing sleep worrying about money (or about children for that matter). Sometimes I worry about money that is needed to help our children, a double whammy.

To my great relief, the funds from all my various pensions have now been transferred over to me. Now I get to start worrying about the return on our investments. We have our LIRAs, TFSAs, RSPs, etc. with a large investment house. Now that I have more time to think about our investments, I'm beginning to question their recommendations. To invest the recent influx of cash from my pensions, they suggested a range of investments that had a return of 2% to 6.5%. While part of me understands the need for a balanced portfolio, I would like to average a return of at least 4% per year. I baulked at the 2% return investment and it was invested elsewhere. However, I wonder if I should be getting more active in understanding all our investments or if we should continue to rely on the judgement of our investment advisors.

Going with the flow

Suzanne and I are now finally entering into a month-long period at home with no short trips planned or anticipated. It is time to reinforce any new habits we have developed and liked, and add some new ones. I'll be dusting off my bicycle soon and will be pedalling furiously to stay ahead of the bugs. Suzanne has many trays of germinated flower seeds that she is nursing along until they can be planted outdoors.

Each day seems to have its own uniqueness requiring us to constantly change our plans for the day. It is all good, so we're finding it best to just go with the flow and see where we end up. It is fortunate that writing these articles provides me with a yardstick with which to gauge my progress into retirement. It's a good way to prevent being unhappy in retirement with no idea how it came about.

10 › Balancing Work and Play

Did you know that retirees with strong work values are not as satisfied in retirement as those with low work values? They don't think their activities in retirement are useful. Unless they feel productive, they aren't satisfied.

In my work with clients, newsletter contributors, and workshop attendees, I noticed a similar trend: newly retired people have difficulty letting go of the puritan work ethic they grew up with.

Here are some of their thoughts on the matter:

- "Here I am, in retirement and still feeling rueful about sleeping in. Still at the mercy of a puritan work ethic. Still not free." [Helen]
- "My ingrained (you could say ingrown) work ethic is clamouring for me to be productive." [Frank]
- "I look at the list of things that need to be done before winter really settles in and muse, 'How did I ever find the time to work!'" [Peter F.]
- "I'm retired, and it's a given that retirement should be far less stressful than one's working life. But how many of us still feel a constant need to fill our waking hours with productivity?" [Brad]
- "When I encounter another new retiree, I am immediately regaled with tales of how busy he/she is." [Rose]

Moral continuity

What drives us to being so busy? David J. Ekerdt, Professor of Sociology and Gerontology at the University of Kansas, explains that we embrace a busy ethic in retirement because it helps us move from a life that valued productivity into a life that is devoid of expectations. It provides "moral continuity between work and retirement." Being busy in retirement lets us cling to the belief that being productive makes us valuable.

When we retire, we cling to character traits we valued in our work world: self-sufficiency, industry, initiative, industriousness, and competitiveness. We become busy out of fear that we'll become indolent, dependent, self-indulgent, pleasure-seeking, apathetic, idle... and useless.

Being busy in retirement provides a defense against the notion that retirees are slack, dead weights on our economy and society, lacking in worth. We can have leisure in retirement, but, as Ekerdt says, it must be "earnest, active, and occupied."

What about play: rejecting the busy ethic

But what about play? Can we not reward ourselves after a lifetime of work? What about mid-day novel reading, lazy bike rides, and hours in the hammock? Can we unlearn the busy ethic?

How do we enjoy leisure, without falling into inertia, and enjoy striving, without becoming mindlessly busy? Can we find a balance between work and play, a balance that leaves us satisfied with the yin and yang of our days?

In this chapter, we'll hear from a senior public servant who found herself doing 130-160 hours a month of contract work after retiring. She tells us of her struggle to find "the equilibrium between the drive to achieve and the joy of living a good life." We'll hear from a guy who has come to understand the overachiever in himself. A woman describes how she is learning to pivot, to remain aware that she is in charge of her next moment. A retired teacher discusses getting fussed about the urge to work part-time. Finally, you'll find an article about how we enjoy leisure most when it is a scarce resource.

Articles in this chapter:

- *Why is it so hard to turn down work after retirement?*
- *Getting to a simpler place*
- *An abundance of time*
- *What monkeys do and do not do*
- *Leisure in retirement — too much of a good thing?*
- *Self-coaching questions*

Why is it so hard to turn down work after retirement?

By Renate
'Retired' Senior Public Servant

> ## Overview
>
> *A senior public servant, Renate found herself doing 130-160 hours a month of contract work in retirement, all the while struggling to find "the equilibrium between the drive to achieve and the joy of living a good life."*

I am relatively new to retirement, having recently retired from my job in the BC government at the age of 55. Most of us feel that we have done enough planning, financially and otherwise, but nothing can really prepare you for totally unstructured time and the freedom to do whatever you want.

For me the hardest part was having no defined timelines. No one checking in on deliverables. No one relying on me for support or guidance. It was super hard to let go of my laptop and cell phone and I found myself checking them several times a day, even though there was no reason to do so anymore. I did try to ease into retirement by planning an extended trip to Europe.

The gift of rest

But still tough to let go. Forty years of working day in and day out, while raising a family, looking after ailing parents, and making a life. Nowhere in that equation was the acknowledgement that I needed to look after myself.

So, I gave myself the gift of rest. I could feel layer upon layer of stress lifting, month after month. I joined an outdoor boot camp. I went on extended hikes with my Bernese Mountain Dog. I started to feel better and started to look after my friends, family, and community much more. And that made me feel better.

The thin edge of the wedge

After 18 months, I bumped into a work colleague who asked if I was interested in some part-time consulting work. I thought about it for a couple of weeks, weighed the pros and cons, and decided to try a short contract —two days a week for a month. It was something I could fit into my fitness and dog-walking routine, and something I could do primarily from home, without long hours sitting in the office. So, I gave it a shot.

Photo: Brian A Jackson, Shutterstock.com.

Well, one thing led to another and, before I knew it, I had three contracts and was working 130-160 hours a month. All different and interesting work, but that two-day-a-week contract had turned into more than a full-time gig. And now I am tired. I still LOVE the work and I don't have to sit in mind-numbing meetings, or deal with human resource issues any more. I just get to analyze situations, solve problems, and provide advice. And I can still do much of the work at home with my laptop and cell phone.

Conditioned to work?

But it is too much. I work almost every day. I am always checking email, thinking about another problem that needs attention. I have gone back to work. Full time, plus. Am I so conditioned from years of work, that I need that type of gratification? Perhaps I am. Perhaps my kind of retirement is to have big, meaty projects that keep me on a timeline for delivery. Is that healthy? I have striven for balance and come up short. Will that change when my advice is no longer current and relevant? Is that what I am afraid of? Or am I afraid that I will run out of money?

I hope that neither is the case. I hope that I can finish up one of the contracts at the end of the summer and work part time without getting sucked into a vortex of work.

Using the years of skill and expertise that I have built up is very satisfying. It allows me to help my kids buy their first homes, it lets me plan for bigger and longer vacations, and it helps me with that structure I still crave. It keeps my mind alert, it lets me talk to other professionals, and it makes me think.

That elusive equilibrium

When I retired, I so looked forward to a life with little to no structure. Time to hang out, have a leisurely coffee, and enjoy a morning walk on the beach. But after only 18 months, I found myself much happier with a more structured life.

I need to find that balance —between mental stimulation, physical exertion, reaching new goals, and enjoying time with the people I love. It is definitely not easy, especially giving up the accolades and gratification that the work provides. But my contracts do run out in the fall, and my goal is to have a maximum of one project on the go after Thanksgiving.

The challenge is to learn how to say no, so I can limit my working day and find the equilibrium between the drive to achieve and the joy of living a good life. I never thought it would be so hard to let it go. Fingers crossed I can be strong enough.

I'm still searching out the balance between overcommitment and aimlessness, still inching towards a new, less driven freedom. – Helen

Getting to a simpler place

By Peter
Retired Primary English Teacher / Curriculum Advisor

Overview

Peter describes how he's come to understand and accept his desire to overachieve, and yet how difficult it is to cut back.

I have always had a tendency to push leisure and pleasure to the back burner, to make sure that the work gets done. That is detrimental because it creates the impression that what I'm doing is work and not fun, especially when there's no time left for the fun stuff. It means I'm not enjoying the process.

As a result of my excessive dedication to achieving success — my overachievement — two problems emerge. One is that I am measuring myself against an external norm, which is not necessarily mine. The second problem is the unwarranted need to do, to produce.

I no longer have to operate in either of these modes in my retirement. The 'doing' part of my life (work, career, reputation) has transferred into the 'being' part of retirement. Retirement means I can enjoy the things I have always wanted to do, but, more essentially, I can simply be. I can exist happily, serenely in my day-to-day life, without the stress of successfully performing or having to produce.

Deviation to nature

I was mulling over how I am all too often stressed and preoccupied — and I stopped for a 'stillpoint' to watch a chipping sparrow flitting around the base of our feeder, near where the clematis will soon be flowering. The thought slowly materialized that I would have less trouble being a bird than a beautiful flower. While the flower is constrained to its plot of soil, the bird gets to travel a bit. After a few minutes watching both, however, I came to sense that each exists in the moment — to enjoy the day and to get some nourishment. The clematis flourishes in its plot, drawing, perhaps imperceptibly, nutrition from sun and soil, radiant and beautiful.

Getting to the flower

I learned from a flower and a bird that it is possible to exist without having to perform. Just be, push down roots and enjoy the sun or the rain; hunt and peck for food and flitter off to a better vantage point to enjoy it. Each in its way is wonderful to watch. Both draw my attention, admiration, and even my desire to care and protect. As Eckart Tollé suggests, they are ethereal, a window into the realm of the spirit. I was reminded of the New Testament description of the lilies of the field, seen as simple and sufficient, clothed in more glory than Solomon, without performing. As I contemplated the chipping sparrow, I realized that I can exist as I am and enjoy my life as well as be enjoyed by those around me. Like the lilies, or the clematis, I do not have to spin and toil, to overachieve, in order to be appreciated, in order to be 'worth it'. But I have trouble getting to the flower, just being.

I feel that with the work I've done on myself in the past months, I have come to a better understanding of the overachiever in me. I have come to accept it and am finding ways to transform it. I have regained an ability to enjoy what I am doing as I'm doing it and not just the final outcome. I can have goals and projects, but they are now there to allow me to feel good about myself and to be the flower of my life. In order to get to the flower, to have time to be a bird, it is fitting for me to be realistic and to cut back, cut back so that what I do and experience is done with enthusiasm. Perhaps I can slowly read my new book, which challenges the cult of speed and busyness. Or perhaps not. Perhaps just contemplate, once again, the birds and flowers and enjoy the day.

— 66 ————————————————

I learned from a flower and a bird that it is possible to exist without having to perform. Just be, push down roots and enjoy the sun or the rain; hunt and peck for food and flitter off to a better vantage point to enjoy it. – Peter

———————————————— 99 —

An abundance of time

Ann Munsch
Retired

Overview

Ann worked as an early childhood educator and university lecturer. She also, at various stages of her life, volunteered with the following organizations: local schools, school board committees, a service dog training group, Al-Anon, and various parenting groups (parent discussion, baby group, life support parenting, older child adoption, and parenting children with FASD). She moved into a retirement community at the age of 66. In this article, Ann describes what she has learned in her many retirements and how she still seeks "a luxurious abundance of time."

Retirement is more like a stagger toward living one day at a time than it is like summer vacation. I've retired a lot — once from paid work, and at least nine times from major volunteer and support groups.

Each time, I saw the choices I was making as positive ones, which would make room for other experiences I wanted in my life. And each time, I expected to have a feeling of a luxurious abundance of time, a decrease of the stress of having more things to do than I would be comfortable with.

Ha! That didn't happen.

Photo: marigo20, iStockphoto.com.

But the recurring evidence from 10 too-busy retirements didn't stop me from thinking that when we sold our empty nest of a house and moved into a smaller house in a retirement community, I would somehow create that abundance of time I had been pursuing since maybe middle childhood.

What I have learned

From this latest experience, and many similar 'retirements,' I think I have finally learned some things:

1. My general feeling of having lots of things I'd like to do is something I carry with me wherever I go. It seems to be part of me, and I need to remember this about myself. It's a little like having a cat in a bag — hard to hold onto, hard to let go of, and interfering with my serenity in a big way!

    Having these feelings of busy-ness, having too many options, not having enough time to do everything I want to do — these mental and physical lists — is not necessarily a bad thing. It's just who I am.

2. Each of my parents left me with a strong belief about the value of engaging with life.

    My mother, when she was turning 70, said, "I think it's going to be so interesting to find out what it's like to be seventy!"

    My dad, a week before he died at the age of 93, said, "I'm grateful I never ran out of interesting things to do."

3. I have consciously chosen to regret almost nothing, and to be aware that any plan involving tomorrow or after may be changed. I can accept that the day will come when I won't want to go all the way to the cottage, and that it's not today.

4. A friend's husband's death three years ago gave me a look, from my relatively safe space, into her experience of profound grief. Of course, this reminded me that bad things happen, we all die, and someone else I know and care about may well die before I do.

5. I also learned to recognize and appreciate griefs over other losses: the loss I still experience following a concussion from a fall at the cottage years ago; my husband's stroke, which took some of his health permanently; his heart attack, two weeks after we signed the purchase of our new little retirement house, giving some desperation to the choices for bathroom tiles in the new place, in between drives three times a week to rehab.

Letting go

About the time we were preparing to move to this retirement community, and dealing with losses in health, thinking about deaths and griefs of different kinds, a wise woman said to me, "there's lots of letting go" in this stage of life. And there is.

I also believe that for me, every day holds the possibility of something interesting — something to do, someone to talk to, something happening, something fun, some emotional investment or divestment. And yes, there are days I don't feel that way; but after a while, that changes.

Some days, in my retirement, I still feel 'too busy.' But more and more, I recognize that I can 'pivot,' as news anchors do when not following the script. I try to stay aware that I have a choice about what I do with my next moment, with my next breath, with my own next list of expectations. Then I do feel I have an abundance of time.

My general feeling of having lots of things I'd like to do is something I carry with me wherever I go.... It's a little like having a cat in a bag – hard to hold onto, hard to let go of, and interfering with my serenity in a big way! – Ann

What monkeys do and do not do

By Brad Morley
Retired High School English Teacher

Overview

Winter is the time of year that this retired teacher starts asking for more to do. He is lured by the notion of warmer locales and starts monkeying around with the idea of part-time work.

I recently discovered a free website called Duolingo which specializes in teaching languages, thirteen of them in fact, including Esperanto. So, we're presently working on Spanish, my wife and I, and I can now say with confidence "Yo como luna manzana" (I eat an apple), and even "El mono no bebe leche" (The monkey does not drink milk). And these are only two of the many and various sentences the website asks me to translate into print or to speak out loud.

You may well wonder why I would ever need, or even want, to know that the monkey does not drink milk, nor eat cheese, nor sleep amongst the horses — all phrases presented by Duolingo for me to memorize, recognize, translate, and speak.

Now in my eighth year of retirement, I find myself once again hankering after some part-time employment of the type that involves two of the things I love: teaching and travel. I've already done two years of teaching at an international school in Saudi Arabia since I officially retired, and I had about a year of several very enjoyable hours a week at a local bookstore two years into my post-career life, but I've been fully and delightfully unemployed since.

Who could ask for more?

I have not lacked for very rewarding things to do at any time since I packed in my 30 years of teaching high school English. Life has been full. I exercise more (and more wisely), I relax more, we're eating better, we share a rewarding and active social life, and money isn't a concern. So why get fussed about feeling a need to work part-time?

It has partly to do with winter coming on. The last two have been brutally cold far more frequently than I care for, and in a mere three months winter will be here again. Why not learn a bit of Spanish so as to facilitate teaching English as a second language in the delightfully temperate climes of southern Peru? Thus, the newfound knowledge of what monkeys do and do not do.

Photo: Anastasija Popova, Bigstock.com.

Is work good for us?

It was an interesting coincidence to me that part of my daily ritual of reading *The Guardian* online recently brought me to a German study on part-time work, retirement, and health (Eibich, 2015). Actually, there was little of surprise in the study, as far as I can see. The subheading said it all: "Retirees take more exercise, sleep longer and need to see their doctor less often than before they left work". In other words, as the title indicates, "Retirement is good for you." As I have said, hardly a revelation.

A key conclusion of the study, however, is that part-time work might help older workers maintain their health. Could I use this study to persuade myself that I should work part-time because doing so will 'maintain my health?' Might part-time teaching in the afternoon of my life's journey be as sublimely restorative as a nap in the afternoon of a wearisome day? Having spoken at length with my brother, who taught English as a Second Language in Peru over two winters now, I know that if I followed suit, I would only be making about five bucks an hour, so it isn't the money that is behind my hankering to work. I do wonder, though, besides the rewards that travel brings, besides the idea of being in a pleasant climate rather than caught in a deep-freeze, whether I'm itching to work simply because there is something about work that is good for me.

Asking for more

Winter is downtime for me, to some physical extent at least. Two of my main passions — running and gardening — are much harder to satisfy in the winter. In a song about what life would be like for him at age 64, Paul McCartney figures that it would be enough to dig and weed in the garden. Who could ask for more? Well, it turns out that, in the winter, I am asking for more. The German study seems to back me up on that, too. Doing a bit less of some things but a bit more of others is probably good for me, both mentally and physically, and the trick is finding the right balance, the arrangement that works best.

So, I will continue my Spanish studies, and though I may never learn why the monkey doesn't prefer to sleep amongst the horses, I can nap well in the knowledge that my efforts to learn a new language and to teach again will be part-time activities with full-time benefits.

— **"**

Here I am, in retirement and still feeling rueful about sleeping in. Still at the mercy of a puritan work ethic. Still not free. – Helen

" —

Leisure in retirement — too much of a good thing?

By Mariella Hoy

My two cats are sleeping on their sides by the airtight stove. The fire is hissing and outside the snow is picking up, wind angling it sideways. The crabapples dangle like frozen rubies from the tree outside my window. While I sip Earl Grey tea from a polka dotted mug, I am thinking about how lucky I am.

Yet, nothing is completely idyllic. A housebound mosquito hovers in my warm space. I have a bite on my face bearing witness to its presence.

The mosquito in the ointment

Retirement may seem an idyllic dream when viewed by a frazzled, fed up, worn out worker, eight years out. Yet, the closer people get to retirement, the more ambivalent their feelings become. A mosquito shows up and hovers in their consciousness. They start to wonder what they'll do with all that leisure time... every day off... an endless stream of vacation days... 20 to 30 years of holidays.

Ha, you scoff! Try me!

I think we enjoy leisure most when it is a scarce resource. I'll never forget how much I anticipated — and enjoyed — my first three-day weekend after 12 months of working without having more than two consecutive days off. I was 20 years old, working as a clerk in a Canadian Tire store.

What would happen in retirement if all our days were filled with leisure?

Yin and yang

We thrive on the yin and yang of things, in which contrasting forces are complementary. Food tastes better when we're really hungry. We long for summer when we're in the dead of winter. Photographs have more appeal when the light is vibrant against a shadowed background. And being enveloped in a warm flannel sheet after being chilled to the core is almost worth the hypothermia.

When we retire — when work is no more — how do we ensure that our leisure is as enjoyable as it was when we were working? How do we create yin and yang in retirement — the contrasting of work and leisure?

I know one person who gets around the problem by participating in so many leisure activities that only the shoulder season makes him edgy... after the golf season ends and before the skiing begins. It works for him. Another person I know has immersed himself in tasks. I don't think it's working so well for him.

And my sister just told me about a retired person who completes all her tasks during the week, keeping her weekends free for fun and relaxation.

Body and mind

Another solution might be to follow my friend's childrearing practice. She allowed her children to choose whatever extracurricular activities they wanted to choose, with the stipulation that one be for the body and one be for the mind. So, her kids could, for example, take up a sport as long as they also took up a musical instrument.

In retirement, if we decide to get in the habit of taking a long walk every day, we might balance that by reading all the books we've been saving up. No hardship there! Or, if we choose to start cross-country skiing, we might balance that by taking on the family genealogy project. One activity for the body and one activity for the mind.

And soul

Perhaps we could take this practice one step further and add the soul: body, mind, and soul. Soul activities are yours to define. For some, soul activities might include being mindful of what is going on in the moment, sitting in the woods, listening to classical music, meditating, and seeking out beauty. For some, self-reflection may enter into it, for others it may be more about getting out of their own head, breathing deeply and relaxing fully. Of course, many people's most satisfying activities, where they are completely in the zone, blend body, mind, and soul.

As one of the foremost yoga teachers in the world, B.K.S. Iyengar, said, "The rhythm of the body, the melody of the mind, and the harmony of the soul create the symphony of life."

Maybe that's worth considering, whether we're retired or not.

I wish I had known that going from a demanding job to unfettered freedom was going to take some time in figuring out the balance between routine and adventure. I might not have felt so guilty about why it was taking me so long to sort it out or making the choices I did. – Anonymous

? Self-Coaching Questions

Idleness, like kisses, to be sweet must be stolen." – Jerome K. Jerome

Balancing Work and Play

How do you measure the success of your days? What do you need in your retirement to feel good about yourself?

What kinds of activities do you participate in that don't contribute to your (or someone else's) health, well-being, or sense of purpose? Can you unlearn this busyness?

How does the value of productivity serve you? How does it not? Are there other ways to measure yourself? Could you choose not to measure yourself at all?

How can you enjoy leisure, without falling into inertia, and to enjoy striving, without becoming mindlessly busy?

Following Frank into Retirement: 5 months into it

The most precious gift

Time. I've got the gift of time. Unfortunately, there is an expiry date to this gift, so I want to spend it wisely. The use of one's time brings to mind many metaphors, some with rather disturbing undertones. For example, my wealth of time could be viewed as the first Europeans saw Canada's mighty white pine forests. They believed that there was enough pine to last over 500 years. It was mostly gone less than 200 years later. Will I have much less time than I think I have right now? In my dotage, I don't want to have the feeling that I wasted my time. Should I be using my time to ensure a lasting legacy? What does leaving a legacy really mean? If I don't leave a legacy, does it mean that I've squandered my time? Do I care? My head hurts. Good thing I've got lots of time; I'll think about it later.

Photo: Suzanne.

Procrastination made easy

It is really easy to procrastinate since my available time to do chores has increased from two days a week to seven days. I've looked at some of the jobs around our home and have left them because the weather hasn't been perfect or the bugs were too voracious or it was just too much work to get started or I just didn't feel like doing anything.

Oddly enough, having lots of time also makes it harder for me to procrastinate. Since I have so much time available, I am very aware of the procrastination potential. Having no real reason not to do the chore (and having lots of time), I just do it. It is a little weird in that the positive reinforcement that I get from not procrastinating makes me even keener to tackle things immediately.

Transmogrifying "should" into "want"

Recently, I was bemused over my reluctance to pursue activities that I actually enjoyed doing, such as cycling and playing music. My first thought was that if I made cycling and music part of my daily routine, then I would ensure that I did both. This past month, I have been cycling and playing my practise chanter and French horn regularly. However, it was not through a rigid scheduling of these activities that this was accomplished. With a whole day to choose from, I allowed myself the freedom to wander into these activities when my muse moved me. It is in my mind each day that I would like to cycle and play music (or cook or read) and so, when the impulse grabs me, I go with the flow. Sure, it still takes a bit of a push to hop on my bike, but it is no longer something I *should* do. I *want* to do it.

This flexibility in scheduling also has benefits in doing those chores I mentioned above. I don't have to cut the grass in the evenings or weekends; I can cut it when it suits me best. No planning is necessary — if I feel like doing it, I just do it. I'm even starting to enjoy tasks that were sheer drudgery before retirement. The grass getting too long to cut is no longer a problem. I enjoy having our yard looking trim and inviting (although if I ever start fussing over our lawn, please just shoot me).

A living legacy

I borrowed the above title from the Ontario government's forestry policy wonks. In our province, "a living legacy" refers to supporting industry and communities based on Ontario's renewable forest resource. My own personal living legacy policy is less clear (those of you familiar with the challenges in forestry policy will realize that means I really don't have a clue). I suspect that this is the subject area that will be the major battleground between me, myself, and, I during retirement.

Are our kids our legacy? We've certainly expended much love, effort, and expense getting them through to adulthood (and will continue to do so). I have all this available time; shouldn't I be doing something worthwhile with it? My ingrained (you could say ingrown) work ethic is clamouring for me to be productive. Wouldn't it be nice to be remembered as someone who actively contributed to the community, helped those in need, or founded an empire?

Wait a minute! Did I just notice my ego sneaking into the fray? If I'm thinking in terms of legacy, then it is basically an ego trip. Maybe it is the word 'legacy' to which I take exception. I don't need to be remembered. When I'm about to 'shuffle off my mortal coil' I want to feel at peace with my life, with few, if any, regrets. I'm not quite sure how to achieve this goal, but I'm positive that it doesn't include words like 'must,' 'should,' and 'need.' So, I'm going to concentrate on "want to do" and see what sort of person emerges. I could be a friggin' saint or evil incarnate. Regardless, I will be truly me.

When I'm about to 'shuffle off my mortal coil' I want to feel at peace with my life, with few, if any, regrets. I'm not quite sure how to achieve this goal, but I'm positive that it doesn't include words like 'must', 'should' and 'need.' – Frank

Three Components for Well-being and Happiness in Retirement

Photo: violetkaipa, Bigstock.com.

What we're aiming for in retirement is to be happy! We want a sense of well-being and contentedness. For some of us, we want even more; we want to be infused with a passion that has us leaping out of bed in the morning with a smile of anticipation on our face. We want that deep satisfaction that comes from being exactly who we want to be, doing all that we want to do. Why settle for beige, when scarlet is available for the taking!

The essential question is this: What will help us flourish in our retirement? Just as plants need soil, water, and sunlight to prosper, we too need certain basic components in our lives.

If you delve into the research, you'll find many, many components play a part in our well-being and happiness, but to keep things simple I have chosen three. If we have these three, I believe we're well placed to have happy lives.

Everyone has a different notion of what happiness is: no pain, love, safety, euphoria, or a moment of peace. Being a transient thing, happiness comes for short periods of time and then is gone. However, we can create conditions that allow happiness to happen more often.

That's why I've chosen to look at the components we need, so we can provide ourselves with more opportunities for happiness and well-being. The three components I'll focus on are purpose, passion, and people. My choices are based on the works of philosophers, psychologists, writers, and researchers such as Sonja Lyubomirsky, Martin Seligman, Alfred Adler, Aristotle, Mihaly Czikzsentmihaly, and Abraham Maslow.

I have learned that most people long to engage passionately in something in retirement. In myself, my colleagues, and my clients I hear an undeniable desire to feel useful and valued, a compelling urge to help others in some way, through our endeavours. Since we spend long days and many years in retirement, it is vital to find meaning, to have our creativity, laughter, and quirkiness spill into our lives and into the relationships we build. Having purpose, passion, and people are crucial components to us becoming fulfilled.

It's not enough simply to want to have these things. We need to first understand the components of well-being. What is purpose? What conditions need to be in place for passionate involvement in activities to happen? Just how important is it to have people in our lives? How do we bring these three components into our lives? How do we create more opportunities for happiness and well-being? Answering these questions is what this section of the book is about.

In this section:

- *Component #1: Purpose*
- *Component #2: Passion*
- *Component #3: People*

Component #1: Purpose

For a multitude of reasons, at times we can feel underutilized, stifled, directionless, and unvalued in retirement, as if we are paddling our kayak in circles. Even when we are generally contented, if not guided by a sense of purpose, anxiety can accompany our busy times and a deep yearning may well up in the quiet times. Have you ever felt that frustration, lack of engagement, stress, and fatigue?

The notion of having a purpose in our lives is not embraced by everyone. Some retired people resent feeling that they should have a sense of meaning and purpose in their lives in order to be fulfilled. They've contributed enough through their long work careers and now only want to rest. Other people would love to wake up every day of retirement knowing their purpose, and having a sense of direction and meaning in their lives. They just don't know how to bring that about. And I've met people who are living with a strong sense of purpose, but don't realize it. They think purpose has to be a grand, world-shaking effort, something too big for them to embrace.

What is purpose?

I think it would help to clarify what purpose means. Only then can we explore if having a sense of purpose can help us.

Aristotle said:

> One's purpose is merely a matter of knowing where one's talents and the needs of the world intersect.

Frederick Buechner, writer, minister, and theologian, said it eloquently:

> Purpose is the place where your deep gladness meets the world's needs.

Martin Seligman, psychologist, educator, and author, put it this way:

> The most profound sense of happiness is experienced through the meaningful life, achieved if one exercises one's unique strengths and virtues in a purpose greater than one's own immediate goals.

Consider purpose as the place where we flourish, where we share our talents — our deep gladness — with the world around us. Purpose is an offering we choose to make. No strings attached. No expectations. Not a duty. A joy to give.

Retirement is a time to rebalance

In this diagram, I've tried to present what purpose means. As children, we occupy the Self circle. Then, as we develop, we find a place between the Self and the World. As adults, we often get pulled too far into the World circle, molding ourselves to the needs of institutions and family.

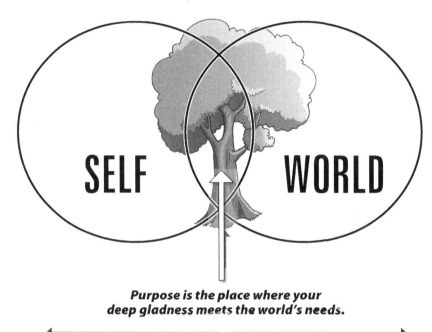

**Purpose is the place where your
deep gladness meets the world's needs.**

Immersed in our careers and families, we tend to overextend ourselves at the expense of our self expression. We don't have enough time to play, to figure out what we love, and what we're good at.

Retirement is a perfect time to rebalance. We can choose to operate with a strong, balanced sense of purpose. That way, we give our talents to the world without giving up too much of ourselves or withdrawing too much into ourselves. This place of balance — the intersection of the Self and the World — is the most fruitful place to be. It is the place where we most likely will find full self-actualization.

Retirement gives us the rare chance to stop. To determine how we want to help the world... be it only one person (a grandchild, a relative) or on a grander scale (protecting the environment, fighting against injustices). We can choose whatever purpose delights us.

Purpose: a touchy — but vital — topic

Whenever I raise the idea of purpose in my retirement workshops, I get pushback from one or two participants. These are the people I mentioned who don't embrace the notion of purpose. They say, "But wait a second! I've worked hard for years. Why do I need a purpose? Why can't I take a well-earned rest?"

Well, it seems that to have a good quality of life (after a suitable retirement honeymoon, of course), it helps to have a purpose.

> *Free time is more difficult to enjoy than work. Apparently, our nervous system has evolved to attend to external signals, but has not had time to adapt to long periods without obstacles and dangers. Unless one learns how to use this time effectively, having leisure at one's disposal does not improve the quality of life. – Mihaly Csikszentmihalyi, "Finding Flow"*

> *A purpose is far more than a good idea; it's an emotionally charged path in your work and life that provides orientation and direction. It's an internal locus of awareness and guidance which defines you by who you are and what you care most about, rather than where you find yourself at the moment. It is from this calling or purpose that you... begin truly 'composing a life'.*
> *– Robert K. Cooper and Ayman Sawaf*

Having a purpose may let us live longer

What makes me sad is when I hear of someone who has given up on finding meaning, purpose, and fulfillment in life, instead bemoaning the difficulty of having to fill up their days, of having to find ways to pass the time. Pass the time! Until what?

An intriguing bit of research suggests that having a sense of purpose or direction in life may allow us to live longer and better, by lowering our risk of heart attack, stroke, and death. In the research, more than 136,000 people, of an average age of 67, were followed for about 7 years.

> *Risk of death was about 20% lower for people who reported still having a strong sense of purpose. They also had a lower risk of having a heart attack or stroke. The researchers speculated that a sense of purpose may help a person better manage stress and encourages a more active lifestyle.[1]*

---

1 Harvard Medical School. (2018, February 1). Finding purpose in life. Retrieved August 9, 2022, from Harvard Health Publishing Web site: https://www.health.harvard.edu/staying-healthy/finding-purpose-in-life [Requires login.]

And, more importantly, our basic security is rooted in the knowledge that we are contributing to the world. Without a sense of purpose, we can feel directionless, as if we're only filling time.

The other thing about purpose is that it can break a cycle of loneliness, the downward spiral into depression and anxiety that loneliness can bring. By helping others, we reach out, connect, and feel good about ourselves again.

Are you still balking at the idea of 'meeting needs in the world' when you retire? Consider, then, the words of Howard Thurman:

"Don't ask what the world needs. Ask what makes you come alive, and go do it. Because what the world needs is people who have come alive."

Start noticing when you come alive! Ask when else this showed up in your life.

Coming alive

The big revelation in my life was the pure joy that came upon finding and feeling a sense of purpose, in knowing my place in the larger picture, knowing where my "deep gladness" intersected with "the needs of the world." Tremendous elation came with this knowledge.

I was 50 years old before I fully appreciated that I have an unquenchable desire to hear people's stories of what they really, really want — their dreams, what changes they want to make in their lives. I realized that, through life coaching, I could formalize what I'd always been doing for fun. I have now had well over a decade working with people who were discovering what it is they really, really wanted in life, claiming their talents, and choosing how they'd like to contribute those talents to the world. This is what makes me come alive.

Ideas for adding purpose to your retirement

The trick in retirement is to find new meaning and purpose, and apply ourselves diligently to our new causes, yet at the same time reconstruct ourselves as less serious, more playful. It's got to be fun! I remember being in the hospital registration waiting line and watching two older volunteers, a man and a woman, helping people figure out where they were to go for their appointments. The man was engaged, smiling, and helpful. The woman was complaining, cranky, and begrudgingly helpful. She wasn't just having a bad day. She made me wonder what retirement tick box brought her there!

We can find many enjoyable ways to add purpose to our lives in retirement. We don't have to slot ourselves into some ageist stereotype. Here are some examples:

- Sharing a passion (e.g., giving free Zumba classes)
- Supporting and protecting others (e.g., speaking up against racism, ageism, gender discrimination, etc.)
- Being a role model: leading, inspiring (e.g., living optimistically with a debilitating illness)
- Passing on a life legacy (e.g., writing our stories, and those of our parents and grandparents)
- Mentoring and teaching others (e.g., helping young relatives choose careers, train for them, and flourish in them)
- Volunteering wherever need exists (e.g., walking dogs for your local animal shelter)
- Sharing to a wider audience the beautiful things you create: thoughts, photographs, quilts, music compositions, videos, poems, meals, gardens, breads, or soaps (e.g., donating a painting to a women's shelter)

As my friend Amy said, "Whether we are fighting poverty, caring for the environment, or babysitting a grandchild, it doesn't matter how grand or how small our purpose. What matters is that we are contributing in a way we feel is valuable."

What if you don't feel a sense of purpose?

Coming into retirement, many of us may not clearly see our unique contribution. What if we don't feel a sense of purpose? What if we long for purpose, but find none? Perhaps these questions will help:

- When do you feel most alive, energetic, and fulfilled?
- What would you do if you had unlimited time and resources?
- What's the recurring theme, the common thread in your life?
- What basic need in your life is not being met, thereby preventing movement to self-actualization (e.g., feeling safe and secure, feeling known and loved, feeling accomplished and competent)? Are you depressed or functioning with a substance addiction?

Consider, also, that you may be operating with a sense of purpose already, unaware. As social scientist Nicholas Lore explains:

Purpose is an ongoing commitment to a principle that becomes who you are...
It is not what you do, but who you are being.

I know someone with a strong commitment to a principle, yet he doesn't see this as being a purpose in his life. By applying his wide set of skills where most needed, he gives great gifts to his family and friends. His greatest joy seems to come from helping others in this way. He, however, doesn't see his contribution as being great enough to be considered a life purpose.

If we value our contributions, however great or small, we can use our determination, our power, and our gifts to improve the human experience. And, along the way, we'll find our unique sense of purpose and, hopefully, follow this Buddhist counsel:

> *Act always as if the future of the universe depended on what you did, while laughing at yourself for thinking that whatever you do makes any difference.*

The world has big problems: racial prejudices, global warming, and a pandemic, to name a few. We are now the elders in our communities. We have experience, knowledge, and wisdom. What can we offer of ourselves that will improve the world around us, in our own backyards, our community, or in the broader world? What can we give, in small or big ways? How can we soothe troubled souls, inspire and uplift, make the world a gentler place?

Living fiercely

Retirement presents a small window of opportunity when we have unclaimed time. Rather than filling the vacuum with what others want us to do, what we think we should do, or with mindless activities, why not fill our retirement with activities that are deeply satisfying, are full of purpose, will improve our health, and will increase our chances of well-being and happiness?

I've learned that, when we discover a sense of purpose, amazing things happen to us and, consequently, to those around us. The world truly conspires to support us. Setting priorities and making decisions is easier, life becomes balanced, and time stretches open.

Living with an iron-strong sense of purpose fuels the contribution we want to make in our lives. Like a hand shielding a flame, purpose protects our small and great aspirations. We're on track. We're doing what we love. We're loving ourselves. And we're giving what we love to those around us. Having a purpose releases an inner brilliance and lets us live fiercely.

Component #2: Passion

As I've gotten older, the list of things I know to be true has gotten shorter. One thing that remains on my list, however, is the concept of flow. I believe that flow — the sense of being in the zone or being immersed in a passion — gets to the essence of what makes us deeply satisfied. It is fundamental not only to personal fulfillment, well-being, and happiness, but (dare I say) to the evolution of humankind.

Of all the components of well-being to pursue in retirement, flow is an overlooked gem. It is about us feeling alive and stretching ourselves in response to challenges, to a point where we experience an exceptional moment. The resulting self-confidence and awe allow us to contribute a happier, more complex self to the people around us. I consider these exceptional moments as passion.

As you read along, I invite you to consider two things:

(a) When does flow happen for you?

(b) How you can create more opportunities for flow in your life?

The effortless joy of flow (the concept)

Dr. Mihaly Csikszentmihalyi, who was a Professor of Psychology at the University of Chicago and a respected voice in the social sciences, laid the groundwork for the concept of flow. He and his colleagues interviewed tens of thousands of people around the world, including such varied groups as tapestry weavers in Borneo, Dominican monks, and motorcyclists. They asked these people to describe what it felt like when they were operating at their best while trying to accomplish something challenging... in other words, when they experienced flow.

No matter how these people found flow — or their optimal experience — their descriptions were similar. People talked about feeling like being in a current of flowing water, or being in the zone, feeling an effortless competence. Although their task was a challenge, and an element of uncertainty existed, they felt in control and confident in themselves. Constant feedback kept them on track. They described feeling completely immersed in their task, losing track of time, and forgetting about themselves and their worries. Sometimes they felt to be operating outside themselves. Afterwards, they felt deep satisfaction.

Examples of flow

Activities that can bring a flow state include playing sports, building things, learning and studying, reading, travelling, woodworking, creating music and art, car restoration and maintenance, creative writing, writing code, golfing, fishing, playing chess and other board games, climbing, skiing, surfing... this list could keep going...

Throughout my life, I've experienced flow many different ways: during hard running workouts; when I worked as part of a team managing the public health crisis during the Walkerton e-coli outbreak; when striving to capture the wilderness around my home in photographic form; canoeing; navigating through coaching conversations; singing complex requiems with the choir; and quietly being in a contemplative state.

The eight conditions of flow

In retirement, we can be happier if we create the conditions necessary for flow to happen more often. In his book *The Psychology of Optimal Experience,* Csikszentmihalyi tells us about the eight major components of real enjoyment, or flow. One or more of these conditions will be present when we are in the flow state, that state of effortless enjoyment.

I find it helps to group the eight conditions into two categories: the first four are conditions that help to create flow; the second four occur during a flow state.

What needs to be present to create flow:

1. The activity we tackle is one we know we can complete.
2. The conditions in which we are working allow us to concentrate.
3. We can see clear goals to accomplish.
4. We know that we'll receive immediate feedback as we go along.

What happens during a flow experience:

5. Our deep involvement in the activity makes us forget everyday concerns.
6. We feel in control, because we are in charge only of our actions, which are guided by skills we've developed.
7. While immersed in our work, our ego vanishes. Once our activity is complete, however, our sense of self returns, even stronger.
8. We lose track of time. Time seems to either lengthen or shorten.

Csikszentmihalyi nicely sums up the value of putting these conditions of flow into our retirements: "The combination of all these elements causes a sense of deep enjoyment that is so rewarding people feel that expending a great deal of energy is worthwhile simple to be able to feel it."[1]

The first condition of flow needs to be looked at more closely. It's the most important one.

Condition #1: The activity we tackle is one we know we can complete.

For flow to occur, the challenge of an activity can't be too great, or we'll feel anxious and worried. Yet the challenge must be great enough to really test our skill, or we'll become bored. The trick is to match the challenge to our skill, but at a high level. We have to keep building our skills as we increase the challenges, until, finally, we experience flow... that in-the-zone optimal experience, that exceptional moment of deep satisfaction.

Photo: Krakenimages, ShutterStock.com.

---

1 Csikszentmihalyi, M. (2008). *Flow: The Psychology of Optimal Experience.* HarperCollins e-books, page 56.

When do people experience flow?

Not surprising, then, that passive activities rarely create flow experiences. Flow is not the pleasure we feel in passive activities like a great massage, a hug, our favourite television show, the warmth of sunshine, or contentment from a friendship. Unlike pleasure, flow relies strictly on our efforts and skills, and not on external conditions.

As Csikszentmihalyi said, "The best moments usually occur when a person's body or mind is stretched to its limits in a voluntary effort to accomplish something difficult and worthwhile. Optimal experience is thus something that we *make* happen. For a child, it could be placing with trembling fingers the last block on a tower she has built, higher than any she has built so far; for a swimmer, it could be trying to beat his own record; for a violinist, mastering an intricate musical passage. For each person there are thousands of opportunities, challenges to expand ourselves."[2]

A red flag for retirees — loss of flow upon retirement?

When we leave our work, we leave behind many of the conditions for flow. Many optimal experiences happen at work. At work, we are usually given clear goals and receive constant feedback, we have built our skills so we can tackle the challenges, we usually focus completely on the job at hand, and often lose track of time, our worries, our egos.

What happens if work is our main source of peak experiences? Upon retiring, will we have activities to replace those experiences? What does it take to completely lose ourselves in an activity? How can we generate flow experiences in retirement?

As I said, we know that people rarely experience flow during passive recreation. Yet, isn't it so much easier to settle into a television show than to pick up a paintbrush or peddle the bicycle up the road? How do we get ourselves to create challenges when it takes so much energy to do so? And why should we? We've just retired from a challenging career. First, I think we need to take time to fully relax into retirement, to completely recharge ourselves. Then we can start looking for things that make us feel good, activities we enjoy.

But what if you can't think of any activities you love? Many people tell me they don't know what they enjoy. Well, it seems that not only do we pay attention to what we love, but we grow to love what we pay attention to. So, pick something, anything that intrigues you, and pay attention. It could be architectural design, or wooden bowls, or orchids. Notice and savour them. That's easy enough to do.

---

2 Csikszentmihalyi, M. (2009). Flow: The Psychology of Optimal Experience. New York: Harper Perennial Modern Classics.

Then you can begin to develop skills in that area. For instance, sign up for a computer-aided architectural design course, collect different woods and examine their grains, or join an orchid society. Not only will you become better at something you are growing to love, you will be putting in place the things you need in retirement to make life sing: structures, routines, positive emotions, engagement, relationships, and achievement. You will have set in place the clearly defined goals, strong feedback, and incremental challenges you used to have at work.

Not everyone experiences flow

Some of you may wonder why you've never experienced flow. It might help to know that not everyone does. Between two to four out of every 10 people never, or rarely, experience flow.

If you haven't been able to experience flow, it may be because you are in a stressful environment. If you're too stressed, you most likely won't want to tackle a new challenge or develop a new skill. If you can't take on challenges or develop new skills, it will be impossible to enter a state of flow. The task might be to transplant yourself to a more relaxed environment, one in which you can thrive, where you are not stressed. Or to enrich your environment — as one would enrich the soil for a stressed plant — so you can explore your passions and seek flow activities.

Finding a passion

If you don't experience flow, it still makes sense to continually set new challenges for yourself in doing something you enjoy. It takes an investment of energy and some practice in focusing attention, but when we do these things, not only do we increase our skills, we find more satisfaction than if we were to participate only in passive activities like enjoying a massage or swinging in a hammock. Our brains find it harder to deal with free time than productive time.

 If you can't seem to find a flow activity, you can do what you're doing with care and attention. It may develop into a passion. Once you develop a passion, a special door will open for you:

> *"And I have the firm belief in this now, not only in terms of my own experience but in knowing about the experience of others, that when you follow your bliss, doors will open where you would not have thought there were going to be doors and where there wouldn't be a door for anybody else." – Joseph Campbell*

Here are steps for setting about finding a passion:

1. Set new challenges for yourself, while doing something you enjoy.
2. Try new things, remember what you used to enjoy, experiment, take note of small enjoyments, and shake up your life a bit.
3. Invest energy and time.

The struggle is to have the self-discipline to create the habits necessary to do this — to build skills, to get off the couch, to put aside the multitasking, and to give ourselves permission to play at something we love for longer periods of time. To be 'selfish'.

Flow and the evolution of humankind

Where does the evolution of humankind come into it? When we involve ourselves in activities that increase our challenges while developing our skills, we grow, whereas if we sit around as idle spectators, sipping piña coladas and watching a dumb show, we might experience pleasure, but no growth. Flow fosters growth. And, according to Csikszentmihalyi, as we grow, we become more complex. Complexity is what leads to evolution.

Flow and Personal Fulfillment

I believe that flow — or passion — is a vital, if overlooked, component of personal fulfillment, well-being, and happiness. It is that exhilarating sensation of being fully alive. Our entire being is stretched in the full functioning of body and mind. We become totally involved in meeting a challenge, solving a problem, or discovering something new. The outcome is that we feel fulfilled because we've lived up to our potential. Although it involves effort, the benefits make it more than worthwhile.

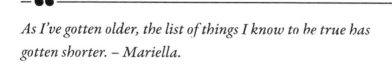

As I've gotten older, the list of things I know to be true has gotten shorter. – Mariella.

Component #3: People

The third component of well-being and happiness in retirement is people. Simply put, we are pack animals; we need to be with people. If we aren't connected, we will be lonely and loneliness is an often-ignored source of emotional, physical, and societal problems.

Loneliness during the Covid-19 pandemic took its toll. A survey conducted about a year into the outbreak showed that 40% of Canadians 55 years or older were feeling lonely and isolated.[1]

Photo: Mariella Hoy.

The hardest hit were elderly people isolated in long-term care facilities. We heard stories of despair, weight loss, cognitive decline, anxiety, sleep disruption, depression, and suicidal thoughts. It was hard to know how much was due to lack of social connection, but their distress mounted with each week of isolation. Being kept from their families made no sense to them, pandemic or not!

---

1 Collie, M. (2020, April 10). More than half of Canadians feel lonely, isolated during coronavirus pandemic: Ipsos poll. Global News. Retrieved August 12, 2022, from https://globalnews.ca/news/6793214/coronavirus-canada-lonely/

Social isolation hurts our health

When we aren't closely connected with people, our physical and mental health suffers. Most of us know this, but I was startled by the degree to which loneliness and isolation negatively affect us.

- Loneliness has the same impact on mortality as smoking 15 cigarettes a day, making it even more dangerous than obesity.[2]
- Loneliness exceeds the risks associated with physical inactivity.[3]
- Loneliness is comparable to risks associated with alcohol. – See Note 3 (Holt-Lunstad, J., Smith, T.B., Layton, J.B. 2010.)
- Social isolation shortens our lives. "Lonely people are 50% more likely to die prematurely than those with healthy social connections."[4]
- Loneliness is linked to reduced immunity and increased inflammation in the body, which can lead to heart disease and chronic illnesses.[5]

In the research, retirement is listed as a risk factor, along with living alone, being unmarried (single, divorced, widowed), no participation in social groups, fewer friends, strained relationships, and physical impairment (like hearing and mobility loss). It only makes sense to take social isolation as seriously as other risk factors, like smoking, obesity, physical inactivity, heart disease, and excessive alcohol consumption.

---

2 Hilliard, J. (August 14, 2019). *Study Reveals Gen Z As The Loneliest Generation In America*. Addiction Center. Retrieved August 12, 2022, from https://www.addictioncenter.com/news/2019/08/gen-z-loneliest-generation/

3 Holt-Lunstad, J., Smith, T.B., Layton, J.B. (2010). *Social Relationships and Mortality Risk: A Meta-analytic Review, Article* 7(7): e1000316. PLOS Medicine. Retrieved August 12, 2022, from https://journals.plos.org/plosmedicinearticle?id=10.1371/journal.pmed.1000316

4 Hagan, E. (2019, January 22). Can You Die From Loneliness?. *Psychology Today*. Retrieved August 12, 2022, from https://www.psychologytoday.com/us/blog/what-mentally-strong-people-dont-do/201901/can-you-die-loneliness

5 Morin, A. (2018, June 18). *Loneliness Is as Lethal As Smoking 15 Cigarettes Per Day. Here's What You Can Do About It*. Inc. Retrieved August 12, 2022, from https://www.inc.com/amy-morin/americas-loneliness-epidemic-is-more-lethal-than-smoking-heres-what-you-can-do-to-combat-isolation.html

We can be lonely even if we have a best friend

Being alone and in a state of restful, healthy solitude is different from being lonely. Loneliness can happen in a crowd. It is a negative perception of being out of harmony with others or lacking all the connectedness we need.

According to Dr. Vivek Murthy, an American physician and Surgeon General of the United States, knowing the types of loneliness helps us make sense of why we can feel lonely even when we think we shouldn't.

He suggests there are three types of loneliness.

1. **Intimate loneliness** is when you don't have someone who really gets you, someone you can let your hair down with and be your natural self. This would usually be with a life partner or best friend.

2. **Relational loneliness** is when you lack friends to spend time with on weekends and evenings, friends you might vacation with or have over for dinner.

3. **Collective loneliness** occurs when you don't have a broader community you can identify with, like a community theatre, an ecological sustainability group, or a walking club . These communities foster loyalty and a shared mission.

Intimate, relational, and collective friendships are each important. Just because we have a happy marriage doesn't mean we can't be lonely. Here's how Dr. Murthy put it:

> *If we have intimate ties in our life, that's deeply fulfilling. But if we don't have friendships with people who can help extend those ties or with whom we can spend time, or if we don't have a community that we feel a part of and identify with, then we can experience loneliness even though we're in a fulfilling marriage or even though we have a best friend.*[6]

Dispelling loneliness

We could all face loneliness at some point in retirement. It is a time of letting go and building new, and loneliness might catch us unawares if we let go of our work colleagues, if our children distance themselves to set up their own lives, if our partner dies, if we move to a new community, if our income is suddenly much lower, or even if we lose some of our hearing and require hearing aids. So, what can we do when loneliness settles upon us like a grey cloud? How can we burn through it?

---

6 Bruettner, D (n.d.). *Next Blockbuster Drug: Busting Loneliness*. Blue Zones. Retrieved August 12, 2022, from https://www.bluezones.com/2020/04/next-blockbuster-drug-busting-loneliness/

1. **Knowing our self-worth helps.**

   Dr. Vivek points out that strong bonds require that we first know our own self-worth.

   ...the foundation of building strong connections to other people is building a strong connection to ourselves, which means ensuring that we know our value, that we feel our self-worth, and that we bring that sense of confidence and groundedness to our interactions with other people. – See Note 6 (Bruettner, D. n.d.)

   Knowing ourselves may require some alone-time to explore our individualism and to develop passions, purpose, and meaning in our lives. Otherwise, without a strong knowledge of self, we may stumble in our interactions with others.

   If we're having a real struggle accepting our own worth and valuing our uniqueness, we could always ask our doctor or a professional counsellor for help. Like professional athletes, we sometimes need a team of professionals to recover from injuries.

2. **Connecting closely with three to five people can dispel loneliness.**

   Research shows that three to five close friendships will boost our life satisfaction. Professor and counsellor Suzanne Degges-White's study concludes that...

   ...the number of close friends we need to feel that we have enough is somewhere between three and five. Not only that, but adults with four or five friends enjoy the highest levels of life satisfaction and those with three close friends are not far behind. And if you have one person who considers you their best friend, the satisfaction you enjoy in life is significantly higher than those who don't.[7]

   The intimate bond is particularly important, because to truly love someone and to be truly loved back, we must know them well and they us. We have to understand their quirks, needs, strengths, values, and they have to understand ours. A really close friend is a person upon whom we rely — in a healthy and loving way — just as they rely on us.

   As Professor Degges-White says, it is the quality of your friendships, not the quantity, that counts.

---

7 Degges-White, S. (2019, August 9). How Many Friends Do You Need in Adulthood?. *Psychology Today*. Retrieved August 16, 2022, from https://www.psychologytoday.com/ca/blog/lifetime-connections/201908/how-many-friends-do-you-really-need-in-adulthood

3. **Being brave and getting out there will help us find our kindred spirits.**
   - workout groups
   - resurrecting old friendships
   - adult education classes
   - local amateur theatre
   - family involvement
   - support groups
   - civic activities
   - volunteering
   - political activism
   - environmental groups
   - book, cooking, or travel clubs
   - faith-based activities
   - dating websites

4. **Getting a pet, while we build human friendships, is another way to feel loved.**

   I don't recommend getting a pet simply to feel loved. Pets have needs that take time, care, and money to meet. However, while working on building close friendships, if we feel ready to meet a pet's needs, then, yes, we could consider getting one. Pets are amazing at helping people to feel loved. Also, some pets can give us a chance to socialize with other pet owners.

Summary

Creating well-being and happiness in retirement may not be entirely easy, but it is straightforward. We are aiming to put three components into our lives.

1. Purpose: Knowing which of our talents we want to share — that is, enjoying helping at least one person beyond ourselves.

2. Passion: Taking on challenges and developing skills doing something we enjoy. This will give us opportunities to experience flow more often, and to grow and become more complex human beings.

3. People: Connecting closely with at least three to five people. If possible, having one particularly close relationship — in which we rely on the other person, and they on us — in a healthy and loving way.

Sometimes our purpose activities and our passions may overlap. That is, our flow activities may end up being what we choose to contribute to the world. For example, your passion for bicycling may lead you to enter bike races to raise money for a charity. Your passion for quilting may lead you to teach classes in the local quilt shop. Or your love of birds may lead you to build and maintain 100 bluebird boxes in the neighbourhood.

On the other hand, our passion may be a private endeavour. I know a lovely woman who has written children's books for years. They remain her private pleasure. However, her passion to train border collies she shares, by helping others train their dogs.

Purpose, passion, and people. If we have these three components in our lives, we're bound to feel a deep satisfaction, a sense of well-being, and happiness. Of course, we can add other ingredients that we think particularly important: fitness is critical. And gratitude, health, spirituality, connection to nature, mindfulness, being hopeful, and making healthy food choices.

As we shape our days, and consider these concepts, I think it important to also consider our great potential. In retirement, we have an opportunity do some good — for ourselves, and for others...

- to develop passions,
- to develop great skills and abilities,
- to create offerings that will benefit those in our world, even the whole world,
- to connect more deeply with people and they with us,
- and to create lives for ourselves that are deeply satisfying.

So, let's tend the bluebird boxes. Paint pictures of water. Make fragrant soaps. Bike up mountains. Console the dying. Capture the morning mist in a photo. Tell that story. Cook for a someone in need. Raise awareness of injustices. Be close to one another.

Retirement well-being quiz

For those of you already retired, how well do you think you are doing? What if you had a scale to gauge your level of social and emotional well-being?

The quiz below is a non-scientific, fun way to measure subjective well-being.

Instructions

For each statement, choose the rating that best matches your level of agreement and record the number beside the statement. For example, if you strongly agree with the statement, put a '6' beside the statement. If you moderately disagree, put a '2' beside the statement.

Statements of Well-Being in Retirement	1 Strongly Disagree	2 Moderately Disagree	3 Slightly Disagree	4 Slightly Agree	5 Moderately Agree	6 Strongly Agree
1. I am content with my new identity in retirement.						
2. I know myself — my values, strengths, learning style, etc.						
3. I regularly engage in an activity that challenges and engages me (a 'flow' activity).						
4. I am guided by a sense of purpose; I have meaningful goals I want to achieve.						
5. I am confident in myself in retirement and know I can meet my needs.						
6. I feel I'm contributing to a world beyond myself.						
7. I have a loving relationship with my intimate partner.						

Statements of Well-Being in Retirement	1 Strongly Disagree	2 Moderately Disagree	3 Slightly Disagree	4 Slightly Agree	5 Moderately Agree	6 Strongly Agree
8. I am close to my family.						
9. I have caring relationships with several friends.						
10. I am involved in my community.						
11. I am emotionally healthy.						
12. I approach life in a learning frame of mind, accepting what I cannot change, and changing what I can.						
13. I have found a good balance of structured routine and leisure.						
Sum of each column						
Total Score (Sum all columns) = _____						

Interpreting your score

When you've rated yourself according to each statement, add up your score for each column. Then total all your scores. Your total score will give your pulse in retirement... that is, your level of social and emotional well-being, at this point in time.

1. **Strong pulse**

   You have a strong pulse in retirement if your total score is between 53 and 78.

   Someone with a strong pulse — a strong well-being score — might say the following:

   I've been going through retirement in a learning frame of mind, full of curiosity. I understand my value in the world and I embrace my new identity in retirement. I get up in the morning full of purpose, open to great possibilities. I have at least one challenging activity I'm passionate about. I've long since given up my old work life and never regret retiring or long for the old days.

I've found a good balance between being busy and relaxing. I'm grateful to be doing what I do, convinced that I'm contributing to making the world a better place, at least in a small way. Family, friends, and my loved ones are a big part of my life. Even when facing a challenge, I am confident that I will get through it. I'm happy.

2. **Medium pulse**

    You have a medium pulse in retirement if your total score is between 27 and 52.

    Someone with a medium pulse — a medium well-being score — might say the following:

    I'm getting the hang of retirement, but I still have lots to learn. Much of the time I'm happy, but sometimes I feel disoriented, like I forgot to do something essential. I haven't completely figured out where I'm heading, in a meaningful way, and, although I don't regret retiring, I have yet to find that balance between doing useful, all-engaging things and the pleasures of doing nothing at all. I'd like to find a way to use my gifts to give back. I'm having a great time catching up with my family and friends, although sometimes I feel guilty when I'm enjoying myself. Survivor guilt, perhaps.

3. **Weak pulse**

    You have a weak pulse in retirement if your total score is between 13 and 26.

    Someone with a weak pulse — a low well-being score — might say the following:

    I still identify with my career prior to retiring. For example, when someone asks me what I do, I often talk about my career before retirement. I miss my old life - the income, the status, and my colleagues. Often, I am hijacked by feelings of sadness or anxiety, sometimes anger. More often than I care to admit, I get up in the morning to a blank agenda yawning before me. No sense of purpose guides my days. The people closest to me are worried about me. My old work colleagues are becoming uncomfortable with my phone calls. All in all, I feel disoriented and unhappy in my retirement, like I'm a fifth wheel.

? Self-Coaching Questions

Coming into retirement, many of us may not clearly see our unique contribution. What if we don't feel a sense of purpose? Or maybe we haven't been completely enthralled in an activity for a really long time. Maybe we're isolated and feeling lonely. If so, perhaps these questions will help:

Purpose questions

Don't ask what the world needs. Ask what makes you come alive, and go do it. Because what the world needs is people who have come alive.
– Howard Thurman

Purpose is our way of contributing to the world... a way of giving the gift of our talents, skills, or passions. Having a sense of purpose gives us direction, helps us feel valued, and keeps us healthy.

1. What would you give to others if you had unlimited time and resources?
2. What makes you come alive? When do you feel energetic and fulfilled?
3. What's the recurring theme, the common thread in your life?
4. What basic need in your life is not being met, thereby preventing movement toward self-actualization (e.g., are you missing a sense of safety, intimate relationships, feelings of accomplishment)?
5. What can you offer of yourself that will improve the world around you, in your own backyard, your community, or in the broader world? What can you give, in small or big ways?
6. What might you do to soothe a troubled soul, inspire and uplift, make the world a gentler place?

Passion questions

When we choose a goal and invest ourselves in it to the limits of concentration, whatever we do will be enjoyable. And once we have tasted this joy, we will redouble our efforts to taste it again. This is the way the self grows. – Mihaly Csikszentmihalyi

Passion can be looked at as the activities that bring us a sense of flow, that allow us to feel 'in the zone,' activities in which time slows down or speeds up. It happens when taking on a challenge and developing skills to face the challenge.

1. Can you identify three times in your life when you experienced flow? Consider flow that occurred in physical activities, hobbies, artistic pursuits, social interactions, group endeavours, and work activities.

2. What sensations did you experience when in flow (e.g., intense concentration, being in the moment, the falling away of worries, a sense of control, time slowing or speeding up, forgetting about yourself and your ego)?

3. What challenges were you facing and what skills were you developing?

4. What do you want to be when you grow up? A mountain climber? Cellist? A much-loved grandfather? A poet? All of the above?

5. What would it take to give yourself permission to play at something you love for longer periods of time?

6. What kind of immediate feedback would you need in order to stay absorbed in an activity you'd like to develop?

People questions

It is an absolute human certainty that no one can know his own beauty or perceive a sense of his own worth until it has been reflected back to him in the mirror of another loving, caring human being. – John Joseph Powell

We could all face loneliness at some point in retirement. However, being closely connected with at least three to five people and having a strong sense of self-worth, help dispel loneliness, prevent illnesses, and improve our chances of living longer and more happily.

1. What can you do to reinforce your sense of self-worth and better value your uniqueness?

2. What would you look for in a kindred spirit?

3. With which people in your broader circle of friends would you like to have a closer relationship?

4. What communities of people share the same interests as you?

5. What supports can you put in place to make it easier to meet new people or deepen existing relationships?

Following Frank into Retirement: 1 year into it (after 0.1 decade)

Tempus fugit

Days, weeks, and years pass too quickly during retirement, so I've switched to measuring my time in decades. Even after 0.1 decade, I still get a frisson of delight each time I realize I don't have to go back to work. On returning from a great sailing and island-hopping adventure in the Caribbean, I felt the familiar downward tug of having to return to work. But wait! I'm retired! Yeehaw! On returning from a busy schedule of visiting kids and relatives, it's great to be back home, but I really don't want to have to go back to work. Superbomundo! I don't have to go to work! The months are zipping by so fast (picture blowing calendar leaves, rapidly changing seasons, and clock hands spinning) that it practically takes my breath away.

The Good

So much of being retired is far beyond good. Even when Suzanne and I are required to do an onerous task, there is always the bright thought that tomorrow is another day and it is our oyster. We've enjoyed spending more time with our family and helping them out when possible. In our first year of retirement, we've travelled for over 0.01 decade. That's six weeks for those of you still on the old system. Our home and grounds are better prepared for winter than ever before. We've even considerably shortened our list of "things that need to be done". However, best of all, I don't have my work hanging around my neck like a millstone. In fact, I no longer need to take any anti-depressants. Proof positive that work was bad for my health.

The Bad

Hmmm. The bad? Maybe the not so good? This could be a short paragraph. I guess I could whine a bit. We can't always be on the move; we also need to spend a significant amount of time at home. I find myself yearning to be home. I want some routine to my days so that I can start to enjoy progress in the many activities that are home based. This was one of the reasons

I was looking forward to retirement. Fortunately, we have the freedom to flex our lives to suit our whims, desires and needs. Perhaps travel should no longer be considered as an escape from routine but as a change of scene, to be used when desired to augment life and spark interest, rather than as a relief valve from workaday life.

The Ugly

There are some ugly aspects to retirement. My lack of routine has allowed my "I should" list to blossom into a full fledged "what would my mother say about it" list. There is also the whole senescence thing going on with me and those near and dear to me. We can dress up our mortality any way we like, but we are on the downhill slope. Should I be concerned? I think not; it's unproductive in so many ways.

Final words

As I have officially made the transition to retirement, I have decided to change my LinkedIn profile from "Maybe retired, maybe not" to "Very retired". My life will continue to evolve as I continue to pursue my second career as a retired person. To those of you considering retirement, I would counsel you to make your plans as flexible as possible and not be afraid to change them continually. There are no rules, just you.

3

Some final thoughts

Photo: Mike Kiev, Bigstock.com.

In this book so far, we've looked at 10 different emotional and social challenges faced in retirement and heard how various retired people navigated those challenges. We've examined how three components of well-being can give us a deeper level of satisfaction, a sense of well-being, and happiness. And we've been probing the question: What is it that we really, really want?

Now, to help us navigate towards a retirement of purpose, passionate activities, warm relationships, well-being, and a feeling of fulfillment, I've put together some quick references, tools to keep handy over the coming months.

In the section:

- *A cheat sheet for tackling the 10 challenges and increasing your well-being in retirement*
- *Steps for preparing for retirement*
- *In hindsight, what do you wish you had known about retirement challenges?*
- *Ten delights of retirement*
- *Book Summary*

A cheat sheet for tackling the 10 challenges and increasing your well-being in retirement

I like quick-and-dirty cheat sheets, ways of summarizing a book in preparation for an exam or, in this case, in preparation for retirement. What can we learn from the retirement tales about those 10 common social and emotional challenges faced in retirement? What about the three components of well-being in retirement — the three Ps: Purpose, Passion, and People?

To answer those questions, I compressed many ideas into a cheat sheet, organized by topic. (Oh, boy. Another list.) Partly my thoughts and partly ideas from contributing writers and workshop participants, I hope these quick tips are useful to you.

Upon rereading this list of ideas, I find they smack dangerously of advice, a distinct No-No for life coaches. So, let us call them tips, those ubiquitous aids you find, breeding like bed bugs, in all self-help books. Better still, let's call them suggestions. Suggestions masquerading as tips, sounding like advice.

A. Tackling 10 common social and emotional challenges faced in retirement

1 Dealing with unexpected retirement

If you retired for reasons beyond your control, find ways to get your head out of the past and into the present. Getting to a state of gratitude for the richness of each day will take time, so be gentle with yourself. Choose how long you'll grieve your loss, congratulate yourself for coming through the storm, and start focusing on what you like about yourself and your new situation.

2 Creating a new identity

In order to create a new identity for yourself, consider what type of person you want to be, rather than what activities you want to do. Spend time getting to know yourself. Discover how you fit in the world, what strengths you have that can benefit others, what makes you feel elated getting up each morning, what gives you a sense of purpose, what makes you feel valued.

Now is your chance to put to good use the power, influence, and talents you've built over the course of your long life. Consider how you want the world to be different because you were once in it.

3 **Rebuilding routines**

One thing you can do to build structure and routine into your days is to block off time in your week for the important things: physical activity, a 'flow' activity, contributing to someone else, mindless rest, connecting with others, and something fun. Take care of your mind, body, and soul. Create enough structure, without rigidity.

4 **Adapting to illness and limitations**

If you've been faced with an illness or new limitation and are feeling frustrated, consider ways to recreate the things you can no longer do, to get the same pleasure, but in new ways. See your flexibility and adjustment to limitations as a new competence. And ask for help when you need it. Others love to help. Keep physically and mentally active — without overdoing it — even if you have a disability, injury, or chronic illness. Physical and mental activity will help fight depression, help prevent pain, and provide a sense of confidence.

5 **Confronting death**

On the question of death... develop a Plan B in the event that you or your partner are widowed. This plan would include finances, housing, bill payment, funeral arrangements, joint ownership of accounts, legal documents, executors, passwords, contact lists, disposal of personal items, etc. Beyond that concrete task, what if you were to view death as the impetus to live life more vibrantly? How could that way of thinking change your week? Month? Year?

6 **Reasserting positive emotions and a good frame of mind**

In order to reassert positive emotions and a good frame of mind after you retire, work on becoming more self-aware so that you can redirect your feelings, attitudes, and perspectives along more fruitful channels. For example, notice when self-judgement, criticism of others, shame and shaming, and striving for perfection show up in your life. Trade these in for self-compassion, acceptance, and feelings of worthiness.

Become comfortable with the disorientation that comes with retirement and stay in this learning phase. If you do, you are much more likely to move forward with greater clarity and confidence. Focus on what is working now and what worked for you in past transitions in your life.

Continually seek out humour, joy, nature, and beauty. Go shopping for delight!

7 Finding meaning and well-being in retirement

Consider what impact you'd like to have on the lives you touch. Enjoy incorporating small acts of kindness, small accomplishments, and small enjoyments into your week. See where they lead. Contribute something of yourself to others. Find new ways to reward yourself, other than external measures of success.

8 Adjusting relationships at home

As for adjusting relationships at home after retiring, have a discussion with your partner (if you have one) to determine what activities you'd enjoy doing together, how big a bubble of separateness you each want (e.g., separate space, time, transportation, television, music, friends, etc.), and how you'd like to divide household tasks.

Build new relationships, outside of work colleagues.

9 Struggling with the creative urge

If you find yourself struggling with the creative urge, maybe paralyzed by fear, consider making a fool of yourself in the belief that your art is for your own fulfillment. Have confidence in yourself, give yourself time to quiet your mind, see failure as learning, and increase your challenges as you increase your skills.

10 Balancing work and play

In terms of balancing work and play, unlearn the puritan work ethic. Make a list of the activities you participate in that don't contribute to your (or someone else's) health, well-being, or sense of purpose. Replace this busyness with activities that light you up and create enthusiasm for what you are doing. Don't get sucked into the vortex of tasks, duties, meaningless time fillers, and work that others want you to do for them. Balance leisure activities with activities that challenge you and improve your skills at something.

B. Ideas for increasing your well-being in retirement: The Three Ps

#1 – Purpose

Find a way to contribute your talents to at least one other person in your world. Yield to that undeniable desire to feel useful and valued, that urge to help others in some way, through your endeavours.

Since you're likely to spend long days and many years in retirement, it is vital to find purpose. Purpose activities are deeply satisfying and will improve your health, and increase your chances of well-being and happiness. So, claim your talents and choose how you want to contribute them.

#2 – Passion

Find activities you enjoy that challenge you to improve your skills. Invest time and energy doing those activities. The goal here is to create flow more often in your life. Flow comes from activities that give you a sensation of being fully alive, stretched to your capacity, living up to your potential. So, play at something you love, for longer periods of time, until you develop skills and can take on new challenges. Only then will moments of flow happen.

#3 – People

Given that social isolation is as harmful as smoking, obesity, physical inactivity, heart disease, and excessive alcohol consumption, you need to connect deeply to at least one other person and to create meaningful relationships with several others. You're likely to live longer and more happily if you do so.

Steps for preparing for retirement

1. Visualize in as much detail as possible what your ideal retirement life would look like.

2. Determine what gaps exist between you and that ideal.

3. Take an inventory of what you've got going for you to help close those gaps (strengths, connections, experience, skills).

4. Pay attention to your conditions of exit from work and find ways to exit smoothly. Have a back-up plan for if your health fails or you need to leave work to care for someone else's failing health. The conditions of exit are the top predictor of how well we transition into retirement. Consider a phased approach, tapering out of your career gradually (through consulting, part-time or project work, etc.)

5. Have ongoing talks with your spouse and family prior to retirement to see if their expectations align with yours.

6. Practise some of the ideas you've come up with for retirement. Research. Plan. Read other people's stories about what they faced in retirement and what they learned.

7. Read books about the retirement transition, attend a workshop, or arrange for retirement coaching.

8. Take action. Now. Set even one goal. For example, I will spend one hour thinking about this! Set deadlines. Look at what might get in your way and find supports to help you. Hold yourself accountable. Have a retirement buddy who will witness your goals and deadlines.

9. Reassess and repeat the process.

In hindsight, what do you wish you had known about retirement challenges?

In response to a survey question asking about the challenges of retirement, I received a wealth of personal insights. If you are now planning retirement, those who've experienced retirement are speaking to you!

The question:

Retirement Challenges: In hindsight, what do you wish you had known about retirement before you retired, e.g., challenges, pitfalls, unpleasant surprises?

The responses:

Responses ranged: the trials of unfettered freedom; searching for who you are in retirement, now that the title is gone; finding purpose in your days; being suddenly without your spouse; adjusting to a fixed income; holding onto 'me' time instead of giving it to others; and balancing laziness with more industrious pursuits.

Here is a sampling of the survey responses:

1. In hindsight, I'm aware of freedoms I neglected to exercise in my workplace. As an academic, I generally wrote within the confines of my discipline. Retirement and the long perspective it permitted to review my life and choices allowed me to see that I might have taken even more control over how I spent my energy and my one and only life.

2. My retirement was a forced one with a change in health. The biggest challenge is learning to live with a significantly lower income than I had when working.

3. Would have simplified my paperwork more and earlier, and kept LESS STUFF.

4. Big picture — figuring out who I am now that I don't have a title and allowing myself to feel, question, and be curious. Getting more comfortable with being uncomfortable at times as I 'wayfind.'

5. Boredom, despite having lots to do.

6. Pitfalls? None so far. Perhaps the only challenge has been allowing myself to not be busy, to not be productive at all times, and to enjoy the stillness guilt-free.

7. Retirement is not for the faint of heart. The complete change of lifestyle is not as "golden" as it's made out to be. I sometimes find it a challenge to find meaning in my days. I sometimes wonder about the purpose of my life now that I'm retired.

8. I never thought I would face retirement without my spouse of 40 years. His death left a huge hole in my life.

9. I wish I would have known that I would move to a new home shortly after retirement.

10. Reassurance that there would be enough money for a comfortable retirement.

11. I should have realized that a "leopard doesn't change its spots." I am now the same person I was prior to retirement. I feel that I had unreal expectations about what I would do once retired.

12. The maximum imposed on pension transfers to LIRAs.

13. I am learning to be satisfied with contributing less to the lives of others. After working at an intense pace for several years in the field of service to others, I am learning to reframe my definition of satisfaction.

14. Getting in shape, for lack of a better term, has gone more slowly than I feel it should have. I hate exercise, so started walking, which I can handle. My calves are starting to change shape and I think that is a good thing.

15. Working friends and family think you have all kinds of time to run errands for them.

16. You are more in charge of your time so it is easy to be lazy. On the other hand, a lazy day can be a good thing.

Thanks to all of you who took time to share your retirement experiences.

Ten delights of retirement

Things to savour, things not common to the work life, things to do for the hell of it

Sometimes we focus on the worries of retirement — lack of a paycheque, not knowing what to do with ourselves, not knowing who we are anymore, pending decrepitude — but retirement brings some kick-ass, seriously good moments. And moments are what make a day, make a life. I thought it worthwhile to list a few of these moments so we could properly relish them.

1. Listening with glee to the morning traffic report, a silly grin on your face as you linger over coffee and a novel

2. NOT going back to work after a long vacation

3. Wearing pyjamas all day long... and putting them to good use by napping in the afternoon (This may not be exclusive to retirees during a pandemic.)

4. Shopping for groceries when the aisles are empty and the shelves full; driving and gardening only in good weather; travelling in the off-season

5. Sleeping until your body tells you to wake up... no alarm clock, no workday morning stress

6. Purging your wardrobe of all unwanted business attire and making room for more true-you clothes

7. Having your head full of your interests and no one else's

8. Spending a Monday on an adventure trip — heading out to who-knows-where to do who-knows-what

9. Finding pleasure in day-to-day chores, which can now stretch out a bit longer without being stressful

10. Spontaneously changing your plans, without anyone being the wiser

Book Summary

My cat is purring and swishing his tail at me as we sit on the couch together in the sun. He is happy that I've returned from a snowshoeing picnic outing. I'm happy that a cupful of coffee remains in my thermos, as I round up my thoughts about this book and my own journey into retirement.

When contemplating retirement — the scary abysses, the heady freedom, and the foggy unknown — I find myself going back to psychologist Rick Hanson's heartening words. "Imagine your deepest wants like a soft warm current at your back, gently and powerfully carrying you forward along the long road ahead."

It may take some effort to delve into our deepest wants, but it is rewarding work. The soft warm current will carry us over, through, and around the emotional and social challenges of retirement. Even simply knowing the most common challenges will help us navigate the turbulence. Here they are again:

1. Dealing with unexpected retirement
2. Creating a new identity
3. Rebuilding routines
4. Adapting to illness and limitations
5. Confronting death
6. Reasserting positive emotions and a good frame of mind
7. Finding meaning and well-being in retirement
8. Adjusting relationships at home
9. Struggling with the creative urge
10. Balancing work and play

The tips provided in the cheat sheet will keep us upright when we run into these issues.

And with some adept dipping and digging, we can set ourselves up for well-being and happiness more often, merely by incorporating three components into our retirement lives: purpose, passion, and people.

1. **Purpose:** Knowing which of our talents we want to share, and sharing those with at least one person beyond ourselves.

2. **Passion:** Taking on challenges and developing skills doing something we enjoy. This will give us opportunities to experience flow more often, and to grow and become more complex human beings.

3. **People:** Connecting closely with three to five people. If possible, having one particularly close relationship — in which we rely on the other person, and they on us — in a healthy and loving way.

Put simply, that means that if I contribute some of my talents to at least one other person, if I involve myself completely in some endeavour that challenges me and helps me grow, and if I am deeply connected to at least three people, I'll be all right. With those components in place, I'm fairly sure my well-being and happiness will reassert itself, no matter what is thrown at me. No matter how disoriented I might feel in retirement, I just have to follow the cheat sheet. I love cheat sheets.

I give my cat's head a scratch, lightly tug his tail, and get up to make more coffee, decaffeinated at this stage, to prevent synapse fatigue.

Back on the couch, I reread the tales of retirement, knowing I will find universal truths and hard-earned lessons from the struggles of the retirees who have gone before me. I find myself cherry-picking some of the many lessons learned, as they apply to my particular retirement situation. (I hope you found a few lessons learned to apply to your situation too.) Here's what I've come up with:

From Jean: To take what I love best about my work into retirement

From Ann: That my internal busyness can be tempered by being aware that I have a choice about what I do with my next moment, with my next breath, and with my next list of expectations

From Phil: That it's okay as I reinvent myself in retirement to recognize that my work identity will remain deep within me

From Josette: To take a moment to sum up all I've accomplished in the career I'm leaving and to celebrate that — with an ice cream sandwich — before moving on

From Rose: That each day is a clean, new sheet of paper on which to write; to remember that a life is made of moments; to balance necessary routines and "the delicious lapse into flow"

From Helen: That I don't have to be productive to be worthwhile

From Donna M: That to build a new life full of possibilities, wonder, and choices requires me to step outside my comfort zone

From Donna B: That it is possible to actually worry less about money after retirement, even if less money is coming in

From Kathy: To acknowledge that adjusting well to a new limitation is an important competence

From Mark: That I may surprise myself by the creativity lurking inside me

Bringing my somewhat anxious personality and ever hopeful heart into the disorientation phase of retirement, I am relying on the stories of those who have gone before me. And I'm counting on the three components of well-being to guide me smoothly from having a career to being retired.

As I said at the start, this book is about getting us safely launched, on a charted course to where we long to be, full speed ahead, and mighty pleased with ourselves. Maybe it's fanciful, but I like to think that the book is a way of lashing our lives together, so we are not alone during the initial passage into retirement. Behind us are those in the pre-contemplation stage. Although they don't understand our doubts and apprehensions, and are jealous of our glorious freedom, they still cheer us on. Ahead of us is a flotilla of retirees, guiding us through the fog with their tales of retirement, raillery, and understanding; sending us new coordinates when rocky shoals appear.

If our brain fog is particularly dense, obscuring our direction and sense of purpose, that's all right. One thing I've learned from retirement coaching is that it pays to spend some time in the place of not knowing, even though it can be an uncomfortable place to be.

Canadian anthropologist Wade Davis agrees, saying we shouldn't despair when in this creative phase of not knowing. To him, despair is an insult to the imagination. He says,

> *It takes time for an individual to create a new world of possibilities, to imagine and bring into being that which has never before existed, the wonder of a full and realized life.... The greatest creative challenge is the struggle to be the architect of your own life. So be patient. Do not compromise. And give your destiny time to find you.*

So, let's take time to create a world of possibilities, to be patient, to not compromise, and to give destiny time to find us.

Looking beyond the unsettling and disorienting side of retirement, I am inspired by the possibilities it holds. With forethought and knowledge, retirement will be wonderful. After a period of adjustment and a refreshing time of lazing around, most people settle into a nourishing way of life. In my experience, most retirees rekindle old passions and develop new ones, learn new skills, and set inspiring challenges. They develop a sense of purpose, warm relationships, well-being, and feelings of fulfillment.

I encourage you to trust in your inner brilliance. To consider living more fiercely than you have been. To consider choosing red over beige. To become passionate about what tickles your fancy. To chew on the gnarly knot of how just being you is changing the world, whether you nurture, inspire, or damage. To muse about possibilities for whatever life is still yours to savour. I hope you can relax into the warm current of your deepest desire, and let it gently carry you forward... once you've determined what makes you come alive, what you need to flourish, and, therefore, where you want to go.

My cat is napping now, chest rising and falling, his purring a base line to the spitting and snapping of the firewood in the stove. The sun is an intense reflection on the snow. As I wrap my hands around my coffee mug, I know I can stop writing now. You will be okay. I will be okay. What was I worried about?

A short list of life lessons from a very old woman

Here is a short list of some of the lessons we can learn from Jeanne Louise Calment, a woman whose well-documented age at the time of her death was 122 years, 164 days:

- Remain unflappable

- Take pleasure when you can

- Act clearly and morally and without regret

- Keep active

- Try new things

- Stay connected

- Have a daily routine

- Accept what you cannot change

- Get beyond your grief

- Do crosswords

- Eat chocolate

Hats off to Jeanne Louise Calment!

The final word goes to Frank...

Following Frank into Retirement — 4 years into it

That's a good pace, now keep it up for another 30 years

Holy toot! Four years have just zipped on by. Who knew that retirement would be so delightfully hectic? But wait a minute, I'm only 62 and there's a possibility that I could still be kicking around when I'm 92. That's a lot of time to consider.

When I was a lad

Let's do some reverse thinking; 30 years ago, I was still working on my PhD and was recently married. Kids were in the distant future (or so I thought). My whole life, both personal and professional, stretched out in front of me and was my oyster. How was that different from the 30 years now standing before me? I can't honestly say that I had PLANS (I'm too much a short-term thinker for PLANS), but I did want a family, a successful career, and the usual material things both big and small. I pursued all three (some more exuberantly than others) and after 30 years here I am — wanting nothing and with another 30 years in front of me. Well alright, it would be good to have a 32-year-old's body to sport around in, but otherwise I am very fortunate to be the person that I am, surrounded by people that I love, and with all that I have.

The one thing that I do not have now is any direction (note that I am still a short-term thinker).

So now what?

Good question! I absolutely love what my spouse and I have been doing the last four years, but my mind gobbles at the thought of doing the same for 30 more years. Shouldn't I be doing something 'worthwhile' with my time? After all, I've got a lot of time.

Let's rule out working for money, as we have enough to keep us housed, fed, and vacationed and I really, really, REALLY don't want to have to deal with bosses, clients, or customers of any sort ever again.

I've written before about being a volunteer, but nothing has called out to me and, truthfully, our 'here again — gone again' lifestyle does not lend itself well to any sort of commitment. We're very involved with our kids and their families, but that is a pleasure and doing something 'worthwhile' has to me the taste of duty and conscience. Not my favourite flavour combination by a long shot, but can I live with myself if I am completely hedonistic? It all makes my brain hurt so I guess I probably will just continue to pinball through life as I've done so successfully in the past.

A silver lining

If I were to best sum up my first 4 years of retirement, I would have to liken it to being a cork bobbing around in the Sea of Life. Occasionally I wash up on the shores of a major life experience, such as one of our children's weddings. Other times I am tempest-tossed by a critical health issue. I have bobbed along in the doldrums and exultantly ridden the waves in days of great surf. There have been so many experiences and such a random sampling of them. My retirement to date has been an incredible gift.

Speaking of silver linings, I earlier alluded to a critical health issue. While it was not so serious as to be life threatening (a blocked artery corrected by a stent — 2 years into retirement), it did convince me to initiate an exercise routine sooner rather than later. Late spring, summer, and early fall, I always get plenty of exercise on my bike getting ready for the annual BOB (Boys-on-Bikes) trip. However, during the colder months, I have always needed some sort of regular exercise to feed my endorphin habit. I was told by the cardiac rehab specialist that, to improve my heart fitness, I needed to exercise (pulse around 110 to 120) for about an hour a day, five times per week. I could have tried to use all those outdoor activities that I do (bolstered with a few brisk walks to our group mailbox) to get my exercise, but I did not want them to become onerous to me. Instead, I bought a used good quality elliptical trainer and spend 40 minutes most days exercising fairly vigorously (pulse between 120 and 140) while listening to news, audio books, or CBC. I enjoy the workout time and any other strenuous activity that I do during the day is just bonus points.

Photo: Suzanne.

The magic of routine

The real bonus of routinely exercising is that it seems to have triggered other activities that I have been struggling to continue or even start. I have found that I am now much more likely to drift downstairs to toot away on one of my many instruments (not the bagpipes — we're still not on speaking terms). Little projects (and some bigger ones) are also starting to get done more regularly. While my preferred exercise time is early morning (because Suzanne is usually still asleep), the routine of daily exercise is more important than following a strict schedule. I am finding that as long as I exercise sometime during the day it has both an energizing and focusing effect on my day. Very cool!

Just scratch it

A cousin of mine was lamenting to me that he can now no longer play racquetball or golf and that his back has been causing him some grief. I feel badly for him, but he should have expected this to happen eventually as he is now almost 94 years old. I know I won't be able to do many of the things that I am doing now as both body and brain start to sputter. Should I be doing more now? Will I feel regretful that I haven't used those 30 years well? I really don't want to be 92 and thinking that I just pissed away 30 years of life.

The real bugger is that there are no answers to my questions. Some people are driven to perform in their retirement, probably much as they were throughout their life. Others become almost vegetative without the stimulus of their work. I can't predict my future and I'm not going to force myself to do something that I don't want to do. So, for the next 30+ years of retirement, my PLAN is that if I have an itch to do something, well then, I will scratch it.

Acknowledgements

In writing this book, I rediscovered the power of collaboration and the joy of creating a product that is better because many heads came together.

All contributors to this book were generous in opening their lives to us, they thought deeply about what retirement meant to them, and they were frank about what they learned. They sometimes revisited dark memories, presenting their experiences with elegance and humour… all so we could learn and be entertained.

Frank, Helen, Peter, Renate, Phil, Barb, and Nancy each wrote a series of articles for the *Retiring with Purpose and Passion* newsletter, for which I am really grateful. Their articles gave me a rich vein to mine for this book. In particular, Frank charmed us with 16 articles, from 5 months before and through retirement day, to four years afterwards. His stories wove a humorous thread through the book.

I would have liked to have included the stories of all those who contributed to the *Retiring with Purpose and Passion* newsletter, but if I had I would have had a tome thicker than Les Misérables. However, many of the 'Gems' and various bits of wisdom came from these stories.

Too many times to count, my partner Mark responded willingly to my plea, "Could you please read this and tell me what you think?" His belief in me and in the value of the project was like nourishing soup to a starving person. He caught so many slipups, willingly joined me in punctuation debates, and brought forward perspectives that made the articles shine. When I was submerged in details, he drew me out of the weeds and into the light again.

Over the years, Suzanne Laytner, Sylvie Vigneux, and Timothy Vigneux skillfully edited, polished, and refined the articles for the newsletter — many of which are included in this book — doing what they could, when they could, and adapting to some crazy-tight deadlines.

The copyright world is a scary forest to venture into alone. Holding my hand were Helen Hoy and Benjamin Hoy (as well as Library and Archives Canada), who gave clear and thoughtful suggestions about quotations, plagiarism, paraphrasing, and permission.

I was hesitant to ask various authors for permission to include their words in the book, but was surprised and tickled when they generously consented, even adding words of support. Special thanks go to Rick Hanson and Marianne Williamson.

In an offhanded way, I asked Barry Millar — an old friend and a professional designer — if he would like to help with the design of my book. For the fee of a dinner out, he astoundingly offered to format the entire thing, saying it was in his wheelhouse. He took all the tiny details that were filling my nightmares — alternating margins, photo resolution, layout design, widows and orphans, and a complex table of contents — and smoothed them into a clean read. I was impressed by his abundance of good humour and patience when I kept throwing changes at him.

Tracey Ujfalussy, my sister-in-law and a design director, delighted me by designing the book covers. She knew exactly where to place the kayak, how to enhance the water, and how to balance the text. I'm thrilled with the result!

I took a picture of my friend Amy Cousineau kayaking away from the dock at the cottage where I join in an annual women's getaway. Helen Hoy produced a beautiful oil painting from the photo and graciously allowed me to use it on the book cover.

Pat Horgan's life and my life have crossed paths several times, from high school days, to business school days, to IBM days. While on vacation in Arizona — between hikes and golf games — Pat read my book and wrote the foreward. I am so happy to have his support, and at short notice!

The first person to read the book cover to cover was John P. Brown, a retired senior partner at the law firm of McCarthy Tétrault. John participated in one of my workshops, so understood my approach to preparing for retirement. He read the book wickedly fast and, in no time flat, I received a testimonial from him. It brought tears to my eyes, for I wasn't expecting to hear such kind and glowing comments.

For the unmentioned, your names will come to me in the wee hours of the morning and I will curse myself for having — momentarily — forgotten you.

Reader feedback welcome!

Thank you for reading the book. The contributing writers and I would appreciate hearing from you. Please consider sending a review through the distributor's website.